LEAN AND GREEN

LEAN AND GREEN

Profit for Your Workplace and the Environment

Richard,
Thank you !
Pamela J. Gordon
Dec. 2007

Pamela J. Gordon

BK

BERRETT–KOEHLER PUBLISHERS, INC.
San Francisco

Berrett-Koehler Publishers, Inc.
235 Montgomery Street, Suite 650
San Francisco, CA 94104-2916
Tel: (415) 288-0260 Fax: (415) 362-2512
www.bkconnection.com

ORDERING INFORMATION

Quantity sales. Special discounts are available on quantity purchases by corporations, associations, and others. For details, contact the "Special Sales Department" at the Berrett-Koehler address above.

Individual sales. Berrett-Koehler publications are available through most bookstores. They can also be ordered direct from Berrett-Koehler: Tel: (800) 929-2929; Fax: (802) 864-7626; www.bkconnection.com

Orders for college textbook/course adoption use. Please contact Berrett-Koehler: Tel: (800) 929-2929; Fax: (802) 864-7626.

Orders by U.S. trade bookstores and wholesalers. Please contact Publishers Group West, 1700 Fourth Street, Berkeley, CA 94710. Tel: (510) 528-1444; Fax (510) 528-3444.

Printed in the United States of America

Printed on acid-free and recycled paper that is composed of 80% recovered fiber, including 30% post consumer waste.

Library of Congress Cataloging-in-Publication Data
Gordon, Pamela J., 1959 –
    Lean and green : profit for your workplace and the environment /
    by Pamela J. Gordon
        p.   cm.
        ISBN 1-57675-170-8
        1. Industrial management—Environmental aspects.   I. Title.
    HD30.255 .G67   2001
    658.4'08—dc21   2001025308

Copyeditor: Janet Mowery; *Proofreader:* Lisa Goldstein; *Indexer:* Ken Della Penta; *Designer/Compositor:* BookMatters, Berkeley.

FIRST EDITION

06   05   04   03   02   01
10   9   8   7   6   5   4   3   2   1

To Gail and Roy Gordon,

*who introduced me to the Sierra wilderness
and advised me as I built a successful company*

Contents

Preface   xi
Acknowledgments   xvii

Introduction *The Myth That Environmental Practices
Are Bad for Business*   1

Part I The Four Steps for Creating a Lean
and Green Organization   19

1 *Question Wasteful Practices*   21
2 *Gain Lean and Green Endorsement Using
   Business Language*   31
3 *Collaborate to Achieve Lean and Green Goals*   43
4 *Track Progress for Environment and Profit*   57

Part II Real-Life Examples of Putting Lean
and Green into Practice   69

   5 *Make a Commitment to Being Lean and Green*   71
   6 *Set Up an Environmental Management System*   81
   7 *Meet and Exceed Customers' Expectations*
       for Environmental Practices   91
   8 *Translate Green Practices into Revenues*   101
   9 *Design Resource Savings into Products*
       and Processes   109
  10 *Reduce: The Best Strategy in the RRR Trilogy*   119
  11 *Reuse: The Second Best Strategy*
       in the RRR Trilogy   129
  12 *Recycle: The Third Best Strategy*
       in the RRR Trilogy   137
  13 *Persuade Business Partners to Be*
       Lean and Green Allies   147
  14 *Make Your Buildings More Energy-*
       and Cost-Efficient   157

Part III How to Make the Most Difference   165

  15 *Become an Environmental Leader*
       in Your Organization   167
  16 *Work with Your Organizational Culture*
       to Support Change   179
  17 *Be an Environmental Activist Using Tactics*
       That Benefit Business   187
  18 *The Fastest Route to Lean and Green*   195

      Glossary   205
      Index   209

The 20 Lean and Green Organizations Whose Success Stories Are Featured in This Book:

Agilent Technologies (formerly part of Hewlett-Packard)

Apple Computer Corporation

British Aerospace, Military Aircraft and Aerostructures Division

Celestica Inc.

Compaq Computer Corporation

Horizon Organic Dairy, Inc.

IBM Corporation

Intel Corporation

ITT Cannon, a division of ITT Industries

ITT Gilfillan, a division of ITT Industries

Kyocera Corporation

Louisiana-Pacific Corporation

LSI Logic Corporation

NEC Corporation

Philips Electronics N.V.

Polaroid Corporation

Santa Monica, California

Sony Corporation

Texas Instruments Inc.

Thomson Multimedia

Preface

CYNICS about the environment abound in business. "Following those increasingly stringent regulations will wipe out our profitability!" they rant. Tempers flare, blood pressures rise, and associations are formed to lobby against environmental laws.

The other side shares this polarized view—that "business" is on one side and "environment" is on the other. Many people think of big business as the environmental enemy.

Yet the truth is that some businesses are saving millions or even billions of dollars each year by taking environmental steps and dispelling the myth that you have to choose between profit and environment. The challenge is for ordinary people to convince their companies and organizations that they can be Lean *and* Green.

Lean and Green tells the stories of people I have met who are leading 20 well-known organizations on the path toward increasing profitability through environmental measures. The 20 organizations include a municipality (Santa Monica, California), a computer chip maker (Intel), a dairy farm (Horizon Organic Dairy), an airplane manufacturer (British Aerospace), and a maker of shavers and TVs (Philips). I personally visited one or more sites at 16 of the 20 organizations; two of my colleagues visited the remaining four. These organizations make cases for "business sense through environmental sense" in Japan, Europe, and North America.

If you play one or more of the following roles in your career and life, you have a vested interest in the promise that being Lean and Green holds.

Employee You work on a manufacturing floor, in a restaurant or retail store, as a teacher, as an administrative assistant or receptionist, in an auto repair shop, in the travel industry, on a farm, as a medical assistant, for the government, or in any organization's trenches. You notice wasted materials and redundant efforts that if eliminated would save your employer's money and be better for the environment, but you hesitate to mention environmental problems or opportunities to management for fear of having your ideas ridiculed or rejected. *Lean and Green* suggests how to present environmental problems and opportunities in ways that business-minded employers understand, so that you are likely to get the positive response you seek.

Manager You are responsible for minimizing costs and maximizing revenue in your group. You want to implement your and your employees' environmental ideas, which will reduce costs or provide new revenue sources, but upper management is myopic about quarter-to-quarter standard performance and you're not sure how to broach the subject. *Lean and Green* helps you gain top management's approval for your plan to avoid waste, prevent toxic spills, and recycle valuable materials. Executives will even brag about you when the Lean and Green profitability you've predicted is realized!

Top Leader You are at the top of an organization. You're under pressure from employees, children, and your own conscience to change company practices, motivate employees to reduce waste, and implement innovative strategies to improve profits while being kinder to the environment. *Lean and Green* helps you to increase profitability precisely *by* making environmentally sound decisions and to then demonstrate these fiscal benefits to employees, stockholders, customers, and the community. If you lead a not-for-profit or governmental organization, association, or school, you will learn how to make pro-environmental changes without risking loss of funding or constituent support.

Observer You are an *observer* of organizations—a journalist, student, educator, researcher, artist, environmentalist, attorney, management consultant, investor, consumer, or friend or family member of someone who works in an organization. You care about the economy *and* the environment. And yet you see harm created by the myth that business and the environment must be enemies. *Lean and Green* gives you strategies for making changes that stick; instead of alienating organizations' leaders, you will make them co-conspirators in the environmental cause—even if for different reasons than yours.

You may have played more than one of these roles, as I have.

After starting my career following college as an *employee*—an administrative assistant at a seminar company—I became a *manager* at a high-tech market-research firm. I became a *top leader* after founding Technology Forecasters, Inc., in 1987. And as a management consultant I am an *observer* of clients' inspiring evolution from costly patterns of use, overuse, and waste to being Lean and Green.

This book introduces you to dozens of Lean and Green role models, tells you what they've learned (often in their own words), and provides a basis for discussion at all levels of an organization. A chapter on ways to generate revenue by taking green steps provides a larger view that may inspire you and your organization to go even further with the Lean and Green promise.

I hope that while reading this book—whether you are at the entry level of an organization or you sit atop it—you will see yourself in the personalities, trials, and achievements of the book's Lean and Green champions. I hope that you'll cheer when you read how Polaroid's Ian McKeown convinced management during a labor dispute to let film testers recycle parts; that you'll smile when you picture Linda Gee at LSI Logic digging out pre-worn but usable shoe covers to wear in the clean room; that you'll be impressed when you discover that for every dollar IBM spends on programs with environmental benefit it gets two dollars back; and that you'll be inspired by the environmental leadership role taken on by Lauri Travis, a former forklift operator at a Louisiana-Pacific wood-products mill.

In particular, I hope that you'll take the four steps toward making *your* organization Lean and Green. I think you'll be amazed that it's not harder to convince management of the Lean and Green promise. It just makes sense.

Finally, I hope that your and your organization's efforts to reduce waste and minimize environmental impact will allow your organization to be counted among those that are Lean—that is, profitable *and* successful—and Green—for the health of the planet and for all of us.

Pamela Gordon

JUNE 2001

ALAMEDA, CALIFORNIA

Acknowledgments

FIRST, I'd like to thank my family for planting deep the roots of responsibility, independent thinking, and affection for nature. They, and their support for my career, continue to help me deliver on the Lean and Green promise.

Thanks to Takako Kawakami for help with research in Japan, Joseph Letterman for his contributions to the research questionnaire, and Rebecca Wilson for her administrative assistance and encouragement.

For their patience during my travels to research the book— and doing well without me—I thank the consultants and support staff of Technology Forecasters, Inc. Thanks go to the author Dr. Eric Maisel; my agent, Linda Allen; and my publisher, Steven Piersanti, for their help in shaping the book to reach every employee in every organization.

I appreciate—boundlessly—the love and support from my

husband, Yosaif Solove. Finally, thanks and admiration go to the Lean and Green champions featured in this book, who combine optimism and pragmatism to achieve outstanding results for their organizations and the planet.

Introduction

The Myth That Environmental Practices Are Bad for Business

> We compare our environmental expenses to the estimated savings that result from the company's pursuit of environmental leadership. The savings have offset the expenses by approximately two to one.
>
> —Diana Lyon, program director,
> Corporate Environmental Affairs, IBM

THE saddest myth in 20th-century business circles was that protecting the environment was the enemy of profitability. *Lean and Green* dispels this myth by presenting evidence gathered from organizations around the world that profitable business and environmental protection go together. Had we upended this myth sooner, companies would have enjoyed greater efficiencies, consumers lower prices, and the planet healthier conditions than when the century began. But we can still achieve all the benefits of being Lean and Green in the 21st century.

The Myth That Inspired a Book

As a successful business owner and consultant to high-tech industry executives, I've witnessed the cost of the myth that lean business practices and environmental measures are mutually exclusive. We cannot bring back the companies that have failed owing to needless expenditures on wasted materials and inefficient production. It's too late to save the jobs of people whose companies could no longer afford to keep them because the companies had to spend millions of dollars on fines and cleanup after spilling hazardous materials. And thanks to action or inaction that resulted in polluted air and water, gone are countless species of animals and plants as well as billions of trees that a balanced planet needs. Our landfills are bulging with slow-to-decompose materials and our air contains 30 percent more carbon dioxide compared to early last century—even in areas as remote as the North Pole.

Yet in recent years I've met dozens of people in organizations who have challenged the myth that they can be either lean *or* green. Some have been motivated primarily to decrease expenditures and increase revenue—the two building blocks of profit—and the environment was a secondary beneficiary. Others primarily have wanted to do the right thing for the environment, and grew successful in their organizations by finding many ways to do so while maximizing profit. Impressed with what I had learned about improving profit and the environment, I decided to write a book about how people at any level of an organization can make their workplaces Lean *and* Green.

I realized that to convince you and other readers of the promise that workplaces and the environment can profit together, I would need to write for the skeptic. So I interviewed management and employees at organizations you know, compiling evidence of expenses saved or revenue generated by their environmental initiatives, as well as the costs of those programs. Here I present enough technical and business facts to dispel the skeptic's concern that, in business, green is a whitewash. The 20 organizations whose Lean and Green successes and mistakes I've included in this book have, at this writing, these three characteristics:

1. They are well known and economically successful (most are leaders in their fields).

2. In the past five years, they have committed no major infractions of environmental laws or regulations.

3. They have measurably increased their revenue and/or decreased their expenses through steps that benefit the environment.

Many of these organizations are particularly good examples because they have made environmental errors in the past and have learned from their mistakes. I chose organizations whose geographies and industries are diverse, as Table 1 illustrates (see pages 4–8). The table summarizes some of my favorite Lean and Green efforts—those that are particularly clever, that include all employees, or that dispel the myth that benefiting the planet and making a profit are incompatible goals.

In this book you will meet dozens of visionary leaders from these organizations and hear their stories about successes and mistakes in finding the intersection of profit and the environment. You also will meet many of these organizations' individual employees who—when they saw waste and missed opportunities—said to their managers, "We can do this a better way."

Totaling Monetary Benefit from Lean and Green Steps

As I prepared to visit the 20 organizations, I hoped I would find enough empirical evidence of the Lean and Green promise to convince even the skeptics that what benefits the environment can also provide monetary benefits. In visit after visit, my findings exceeded even my own expectations. Here are just a few:

(continued on page 8)

Table 1   The 20 Lean and Green Organizations
with Stories in This Book

Organization and Website URL	Sites Visited (products, services)	My Favorite Lean and Green Stories
Agilent Technologies (formerly part of Hewlett-Packard) www.agilent.com	South Queensferry, Scotland (tele-communications)	Security guards wrote "nasty" notes to employees to encourage them to turn off computer screens at night; the result: 400 megawatts hours of electricity saved per year.
Apple Computer Corporation www.apple.com	Sacramento, California, USA (computer products)	Team Recycle drove Apple to recycle—which it now does for 97.3 percent of all incoming materials.
British Aerospace, Military Aircraft & Aerostructures Division www.bae.co.uk	Samlesbury, England (aircraft)	The company adopted an at-home environmental program, including a quiz written by an employee about Lean and Green shopping.
Celestica Inc. www.celestica.com	Toronto, Canada (electronics manu-facturing services)	Instead of replacing ozone-depleting cleaners with water cleaners, they made the whole cleaning process unnecessary.
Compaq Computer Corporation www.compaq.com	Houston, Texas, USA (personal computers)	Architects designed buildings with skylights, to significantly reduce electricity use.

(continued)

Table 1   *(continued)*

Organization and Website URL	*Sites Visited (products, services)*	*My Favorite Lean and Green Stories*
Horizon Organic Dairy, Inc. www.horizonorganic .com	Paul, Idaho, and Annapolis Maryland, USA (dairy farm)	Through organic farming and by treating the cows better, the company eliminated the need to buy chemicals, hormones, or fertilizers.
IBM Corporation www.ibm.com	Endicott, New York, USA (printed-circuit boards)	By developing a method to reuse etchant chemicals through contact with oxygen-rich air, the company reduced its use of etchants by 50 million gallons a year.
Intel Corporation www.intel.com	Chandler, Arizona, USA (semiconductors)	Designing green manufacturing processes for products to be released 8 to 12 years into the future reduces the need to buy abatement equipment or get permits for hazardous processes that otherwise would have been used in the interim.
ITT Cannon, a division of ITT Industries www.ittcannon.com	Santa Ana, California, USA (connectors for ships, airplanes, etc.)	Employees convinced the military to use degreasers that do not deplete the ozone and that cost less.

(continued)

Table 1　*(continued)*

Organization and Website URL	Sites Visited (products, services)	My Favorite Lean and Green Stories
ITT Gilfillan, a division of ITT Industries www.gilfillan.itt.com	Van Nuys, California, USA (radar)	This company developed a method of labeling parts using a computer printer instead of smelly, hazardous paints.
Kyocera Corporation www.kyocera.co.jp	Tokyo, Japan (printers)	Designers developed printers that cost less to use and have fewer parts to replace.
Louisiana-Pacific Corporation www.lpcorp.com	Hines, Oregon, USA (wood products for building supplies)	Management overhauled the corporate culture, teaching employees to communicate with management and teaching management to value decisions that are environmentally sound.
LSI Logic Corporation www.lsil.com	Gresham, Oregon (custom semiconductors for communications products)	By reusing water in the production facility, the manufacturing process needs 63 percent less water than it did before.
NEC Corporation www.nec-global.com	Tokyo, Japan (semiconductors and consumer electronics)	The company's "zero waste" program is saving 0.2 percent in product costs.

(continued)

Table 1   *(continued)*

Organization and Website URL	Sites Visited (products, services)	My Favorite Lean and Green Stories
Philips Electronics N.V. www.philips.com	Eindhoven and Nijmegen, Holland (semiconductors for televisions, shavers, and other products)	Employees who design environmentally sound products and manage plants with Lean and Green results are eligible to win the company's EcoVision award.
Polaroid Corporation www.polaroid.com	Dumbarton, Scotland (cameras)	After redesigning the product assembly process to nearly eliminate wasted materials, the cost of manufacturing was reduced by 20 percent.
Santa Monica www.santa-monica.ca.us	Santa Monica, California, USA (city government)	This city was the first on the West Coast to pave residential streets with white-top, which is stronger and thinner than black asphalt, reduces urban heat by 15 degrees on the street level, lasts 50 years instead of 5, and costs just a little more to install.
Sony Corporation www.sony.com	Tokyo, Japan (sound systems and other products)	The company recycles sludge to make cement and has implemented other waste-less and recycle-more ideas; waste disposed of per unit of sales fell 30 percent in four years.

(continued)

Table 1   *(continued)*

Organization and Website URL	Sites Visited (products, services)	My Favorite Lean and Green Stories
Texas Instruments Incorporated www.ti.com	Dallas, Texas, USA (semiconductors)	Having planned to design-out hazardous materials in 6 to 12 months, employees eliminated the use of 49 of 50 hazardous chemicals in only 2 months.
Thomson Multimedia www.thomson-multi media.com	Boulogne, France (televisions and other consumer products)	Scientists improved the plastic for television cabinets to eliminate not only any caustic paints but also the entire expensive and time-consuming painting process.

► Texas Instruments' reduction of hazardous waste by 44 percent has an enormous impact on profitability and productivity. The company recycles 81 percent of nonhazardous solid waste in its U.S. operations (and 75 percent worldwide), which saves $23 million worth of water and energy, not to mention saving trees and reducing landfill. TI spends $160 million on manufacturing resources each quarter; the environmental programs are designed to optimize the company's resources by at least 10 percent—to save at least $16 million each quarter. Actually, TI's environmental achievement at this writing has exceeded the 10 percent target.

► LSI Logic's environmental programs have saved the company more than $2 million. LSI has significantly reduced its use of hazardous manufacturing chemicals such as sulfuric acid, photoresist, and phosphoric acid, saving the company $1.2 million alone. The company has reduced its total volume of hazardous waste by 88 percent since 1987.

▶ NEC Semiconductor's environmental protection plan generates 0.2 percent of its total semiconductor sales in cost savings and recycling revenues.

▶ Thomson Multimedia's worldwide environmental projects yield the company $12.5 million each year through cost avoidance, cost savings, and revenue generation. Waste reclamation and glass recycling (from TV CRTs) contribute the most toward the $12.5 million. By reducing electricity, fuel, and gas in Europe alone the company saves $2.8 million.

▶ Sony's U.S. operations generated $1.8 million by reducing industrial waste (36,000 tons of industrial waste, including printed-circuit boards and office paper) and reduced electricity use by $1.3 million.

▶ Polaroid in Scotland saves £3.8 million (nearly $6 million) per year by creatively reusing (and eventually recycling) suppliers' shipping boxes.

▶ Philips has saved more than 1 billion Dutch guilders (more than $400 million) per year by reducing waste 28 percent, energy use 23 percent, and water use 34 percent. Philips saved 17 percent more than it had originally projected.

▶ ITT Cannon: Cost savings from replacing ozone-depleting chlorofluorocarbon (CFC) solvents with water-soluble solutions are close to $1 million each year.

► The city of Santa Monica, in addition to its white-top *street* success above, is saving $50,000 a year by using an innovative application of small paving materials for *sidewalk* repairs. Street maintenance employees developed this idea, which saves time, labor, and materials and reduces waste.

► British Aerospace: Samlesbury shop-floor employees' efforts to find environmentally friendly improvements that make their processes leaner yielded £480,000 (more than $700,000) savings per year.

And what about revenue gain? Some of the best-selling products of Lean and Green organizations, such as Horizon Organic Dairy and Louisiana-Pacific, were created to minimize waste, chemicals, and unnecessary transportation. Yes, green products designed to meet customer needs do sell well.

Another critical type of monetary benefit of Lean and Green thinking is protecting an organization's good reputation. Fear of violating environmental regulations motivated executives at chip maker LSI Logic to insist on a strong environmental department. Wilfred Corrigan, LSI Logic's chief executive officer, was one of the presidents of Fairchild, an early semiconductor company that generated significant environmental problems. During LSI's formative years in the early 1980s, the semiconductor industry was prominent on lists of polluting companies. Linda Gee, environmental health and safety director at LSI, told me, "I still have the memo Joe Zelayeta, executive vice president of worldwide operations, sent me when I started with LSI. It was a list of non-compliant companies that had discharged wastewater to the City of San Jose Sewer Plant. Joe wrote, 'Congratulations, this is a great list *not* to be a part of. I know you seldom get any notoriety except when you have a problem, so I think you should get credit for avoiding the dishonor roll in the *San Jose Mercury News.* Thanks!'" Linda has kept LSI off the lists and in the black through her dogged attention to waste reduction and reuse of materials.

But How Much Is *Spent* on Environment Steps?

According to the lean *or* green myth, environmental concerns take resources away from business, and time and funds diverted from narrow-enough profit margins will take business off course. Actually, the reverse is true: IBM, for example, estimates that for every dollar spent on environmental benefit or pollution prevention, two dollars are added to the bottom line.

Intel participates in a benchmarking study with Pricewater-houseCoopers to determine the cost to organizations of their environment, health, and safety (EHS) organization—the number of EHS employees per billion dollars of revenue. Intel's cost is among the lowest in the sample, and the by-product of its environmental programs is reduced operational costs and getting new products to the market faster by fulfilling and going beyond environmental-permit standards.

Linda Gee at LSI Logic says that many environmental program expenditures—such as for on-site recycling equipment through which used chemicals are passed, then used again—make money for the company in less than one year.

Polaroid's savings of £3.8 million (nearly $6 million) from its reusable-box program does require paying four times more per box for the reusable shipping boxes (£4) than it paid for cardboard boxes (£1). The original plan was that after reusing the same box for four trips, Polaroid would break even. Polaroid stopped counting the return trips after the boxes exceeded 64 trips, and the company estimates that many boxes have made more than 500 trips before being recycled. Even including the cost of shipping flats of the reusable boxes back to suppliers in Mexico and Malaysia, savings exceed ship-back costs hundreds of times.

Four Lean and Green Steps for the Biggest Impact

I want to make it as easy as possible for you to make quick, effective changes in your workplace for the improvement of our natural environment while strengthening your organization. So, I am giving you the four fastest steps to Lean and Green (listed in sidebar). I synthesized these four steps after witnessing results at the Lean and Green organizations and asking the Lean and Green champions I visited around the world which techniques had produced the most cost savings or revenue *and benefited the environment*.

Chapters 1 through 4 guide you through these four steps. Then, the rest of this book's chapters present real-life stories that provide inspiration for making the four steps work at *your* organization. They include practical suggestions for what *you* can do in *this* century to help produce a win-win outcome: successful business practices and a healthy planet.

Four Steps to Lean and Green

1. **Question wasteful practices, and design Lean and Green steps to benefit profit and planet.** Get people in your organization to think creatively in order to arrive at Lean and Green solutions; for the most dramatic benefits, encourage them to think about steps that can be taken *before* waste is created.

2. **Gain endorsement for Lean and Green ideas using business language.** Lead your environmental points with profit in mind — starting with strategies that yield the highest rewards to profit and planet.

3. **Collaborate throughout the organization to meet Lean and Green goals.** If you can, start at the top of the organization to obtain buy-in there, then adopt the Lean and Green practices elsewhere in the organization.

4. **Measure your organization's Lean and Green progress, and strive continuously to improve.** Make sure that the Lean and Green steps your organization is taking are truly healthful both for planet and for profit, and keep raising the bar.

Competition Is Doing Its Job

Leaders who think that what is good for the environment is bad for business are at a competitive disadvantage. Their profit margins are several points lower because they purchase and dispose of excess materials and pay for waste that needn't have been created in the first place. They forgo revenue from recycling (such as Apple's gain of $1 million) and from marketing "green" products (such as Philips's popular GreenChip™). They take unnecessary processing steps and pay sick leave and health care costs when employees are exposed to ill-chosen chemicals. Some of these leaders' organizations have leaked toxins into the groundwater and polluted the air—resulting in millions of dollars in fines and cleanup costs. Had these inefficiencies been avoided and accidents been prevented by sound environmental policies, their earnings would have been much higher.

By taking environmental steps, many of the Lean and Green organizations are shaving 1 to 15 percent and more off costs. These savings can allow them to reduce prices—a move that usually increases market share—or earn higher profits if prices are held steady.

As *Lean and Green* organizations outperform those that are buying too much, wasting what they buy, and missing green revenue opportunities, more stakeholders will insist on changes. Note how my Lean and Green contacts achieve competitive advances by making environmental improvements in their organizations.

▶ Danny Martland is environmental advisor at British Aerospace's Samlesbury facility. He observes that his site "is renowned for lean manufacturing to survive in the world market. We've already looked with a fine-tooth comb to make machines more efficient and cut out waste. Then in only 12 months of getting people interested in making environmental improvements, we achieved nearly an additional £500,000 of efficiency."

▶ David Lear, environmental program manager at Compaq, says, "It's hard to put a price on avoiding liability, but I try to do so by looking at financial and environmental reports for what our competitors have spent to correct environmental mistakes: some electronics companies have spent upwards of $150 million in one year. Think of the number of computers they'd have to sell to earn back that money in profits! We also look at other companies' employee count and departments assigned to clean up environmental mistakes. Our group is lean because we've not had environmental mistakes to clean up."

▶ Walt Rosenberg is director of corporate environmental affairs at Compaq, where, on a per-product basis in the competitive personal computer market, he says, "even 1 percent cost savings is motivational. We're fighting on pennies on some components—because pennies count when multiplied by millions of units. The mindset is 'every single cent.' A reusable transport pallet saves $5 per unit—this becomes a fundamental business benefit."

▶ Bob Barrett, an environmental and material engineer at ITT Gilfillan, notes that the radar market is very competitive right now. "When we improve radar design so they are smaller, lighter, more efficient, and more reliable, and use fewer materials, less coolant, less power, and less space, and use fewer chemicals with associated complications, we get a competitive edge."

▶ Frank O'Rourke is the EHS manager at Celestica. He looks for every possible way to save money because, in Celestica's industry—electronics manufacturing services—profit margins are small. The main reason name-brand companies outsource manufacturing to companies like his is to reduce costs.

Becoming Lean and Green Table 3 provides a few typical "before and after" stories about Lean and Green organizations. *You* can help create an "after" picture for the organizations you know.

Table 3 Company Practices Before and After Lean and Green		
	Before Lean and Green	*After Lean and Green*
Purchases	Buying, storing, and managing more materials than really needed; paying higher bills for energy and water.	Eliminating some purchases by designing processes and products that save steps, time, materials, and square footage; reducing other purchases by reusing existing materials.
Disposal	Paying freight and handling to dispose of materials that could have been avoided, reused, or recycled; obtaining and renewing time-consuming and expensive permits for disposing of hazardous materials.	Paying less for disposal because much less is wasted; earning revenues through recycling.
Transportation	Paying more for transportation of incoming materials and hauling waste.	Using less transportation by processing and packaging and reducing the quantity of materials flowing into and out of each site.

(continued)

Table 3   Company Practices Before and After Lean and Green

	Before Lean and Green	*After Lean and Green*
Labor	Excessive hiring to maintain wasteful procedures; watching absences and illness rise owing to exposure to unnecessary chemicals.	Employees reporting fewer headaches and other illnesses and accidents; morale increases through the pride of working for a Lean and Green organization.
Cleanup and Fines	Cleaning up spills and paying penalties of millions of dollars; damaged reputations and even prison sentences.*	Incurring no costs for cleanup or fines; strengthening reputations by processing wastes properly.
Revenues	Losing market share to competitors who use material and energy efficiencies to offer less expensive products or products that have a smaller impact on the planet.	Earning greater market share by introducing efficiencies that allow prices of products to be reduced; offering innovative products that reduce operational costs and meet customers' increasing "green" standards.
Bottom Line	Higher expenses and lower revenues = LESS PROFIT	Lower expenses and higher revenues = MORE PROFIT

*As occurred at one of the twenty organizations before it became Lean and Green.

You Can Transform Your Organization

In this book, I introduce you to clerks, farmers, lumber mill workers, engineers, city employees, chemists, managers, and executives. They work for 20 successful organizations all over the world. You will read about their successes and mistakes as they strived to make their organizations healthier financially and more productive for employees, the community, and the planet. All of them have made a discovery: Lean and Green can coexist because what's good for business—less waste and fewer production steps—is good for the environment too.

I invite you to be receptive to the idea that it's possible for you to make the organizations you touch Lean and Green.

Part I
The Four Steps
for Creating a Lean and Green Organization

THIS part of the book provides you with the basics: the four Lean and Green steps, which are helpful to memorize, and some ideas about how to take each one.

Step 1. Question wasteful practices, and design Lean and Green steps to benefit profit and planet.

Step 2. Gain endorsement for Lean and Green ideas using business language.

Step 3. Collaborate throughout the organization to meet Lean and Green goals.

Step 4. Measure your organization's Lean and Green progress, and strive continuously to improve.

When I make a list of what I want most in life, I start it with the wish that the planet have clean air and clean water. To me, everything else pales in comparison. Also on my list is continued success in my career as a management consultant in the high-tech and environmental fields. I get tremendous satisfaction from helping executives to increase the profitability of their businesses.

Those two goals are my biggest motivation for writing this book to convince you that you can make improvements—right away and with less effort than you might think—to the health of the environment and your business or organization. The four Lean and Green steps featured in Chapters 1 through 4 are the best way I know of to achieve the Lean and Green promise in your workplace.

Chapter 1
Question Wasteful Practices

The groundswell associated with the environment is changing industry. Employees who completed school 10 and fewer years ago ask their managers, "Why are we doing such and such a thing?" They're bringing in waste-reduction ideas.

—Ian McKeown, senior engineer
of Health, Safety, and Environment, Polaroid

THIS chapter focuses on the first of the four Lean and Green steps: Question wasteful practices, and design Lean and Green steps to benefit profit and planet. Get people in your organization to think creatively to arrive at Lean and Green solutions; for the most dramatic benefits, encourage them especially to think about steps *before* waste is created. Many of the Lean and Green companies' best ideas for cost savings and environmental good come from employees without "environment" or "manager" anywhere in their titles. Let your creativity soar. Your idea could save money, trees, or likely both.

One of the reasons I wrote this book is to make more people aware of the tremendous impact organizations can have on the planet and its inhabitants' health—both positively and negatively. Think about this: You and I can reduce waste at home and recycle our newspapers, cans, bottles, and paper. In fact, doing so happens to be my favorite household chore because I know that these items will not contribute to local landfills, which in my community are filling up the beautiful San Francisco Bay. Yet you and I can reduce the use of landfills and incinerators in several communities—perhaps around the world—when we create waste-reduction strategies for our organizations. This truly is a faster and more effective way to curb and reverse the trend on our planet to waste more and more resources.

At IBM, for example, which has dozens of manufacturing sites and hundreds of sales and administrative offices worldwide, individual employees at all levels have helped to improve the environment while benefiting IBM's business. One employee's idea to give each employee a ceramic mug is reducing the company's use of paper and styrofoam each year. In addition to providing an environmental benefit, IBM's suggestion program gives its employees a percentage of the cost savings that result from their ideas.

Notice and Question

Employees in the trenches—those with customer contact, who order materials, and who build products—often are better positioned than management to notice practices that can be improved and to question why things are done a certain way. Wherever you work, pay attention to what chemicals, energy, and supplies your company buys that could be eliminated with only a few changes.

Here's an example of how individual employees are encouraged to notice and question usual practices: Henk de Bruin at Philips told me that employees at a new factory wanted the plant to meet the environmental standard set by ISO 14000 (see Glossary) by the time it started manufacturing products: "So the factory simply created environmental-action teams in each department who asked all employees in the plant, 'Suppose that in your day-to-day work you want to decrease negative impact on the environment, how would you do it?' Someone said, 'Let's use as many as four receptacles for paper, cans, and other recyclable trash.' Another said, 'Why don't we use coffee mugs instead of disposable cups?' The factory employed these ideas in the six months it took to get the factory started." De Bruin emphasized the importance of employee suggestions: "We establish improvement targets at the corporate level, but the filling in of ideas to meet these targets has to be from the bottom up."

Some Lean and Green solutions seem so obvious, but they took at least one employee to notice the waste or pollution and create a new way. ITT Cannon is making good use of some old machines, but they leak oil. The company used to spend $50,000 a year on kitty litter, which it spread on the floor around the leaking equipment to absorb the oil, and then incinerated. Since one employee questioned this expensive, environmentally questionable, and messy practice, Cannon has eliminated the kitty litter and instead is using pans under the machines to catch the oil drips; the oil is then vacuumed up and resold.

How would you like to save your company $20 million? The Packaging and Commodity Logistics Team at Texas Instruments examines how TI packages its products for shipment around the world. It considers whether materials that are thrown away could instead be recycled, reused, or eliminated. Shaunna Sowell says, "The team asks, 'Why are we doing it this way? Why can't we do it better?'" In three years the team saved TI $20 million in real costs by doing such things as getting suppliers to return packaging materials so TI doesn't have to buy them. Says Sowell, "We make people clear on what the enemy is and turn people's creativity loose on it."

A suggestion made by a team of three machine operators at

British Aerospace is saving the company £30,000 per year. They noticed that the vapor-degreasing machine ran 24 hours a day, consuming 18,000 liters of solvent and creating unsatisfactory emission levels. They questioned why the equipment had to run all the time. Danny Martland explained, "First the team decided to cut off the nightshift emissions. Then they said, 'Let's use an automatic timer to do it just two hours a day.' They found a way to improve the degreasing method by dipping parts in the tank and then raising them slowly." The environmental and cost savings resulted from controlling the degreaser operating times, fitting an automatic timer, creating new timetables for operating the degreaser, and training operators how to improve degreasing methods. The cost of implementing this change was a one-time charge of £50. Solvent use was reduced from eight barrels per week to only three, and emissions decreased by 60 percent. For creating this idea, the three operators split a £5,000 award. Danny says, "The operators on the process were putting into action part of our ethics—getting people involved. We tell employees that we look very favorably on the environmental suggestions put in the suggestion box."

Danny Martland at British Aerospace stresses the effectiveness of training employees in environmental process improvement and encouraging them to create ideas. He says, "If without this training an engineer had asked the team of three operators to make the degreasing process more efficient, the operators would not have been able to do so." An environmental coordinator at each plant helps employees develop their ideas.

Ideas to Spark *Your* Imagination

"All right," some of you are thinking, "I'm convinced from all these examples that a person could notice pollution or waste in his or her organization, question the usual procedures, and think of a way that cleans up or prevents the waste, which means lower expenses for the company. But I'm not an expert in the environment, and I'm not particularly creative." (And if you're also thinking, "Furthermore, how could I convince management to make the change?" hold on to that question—you'll see in the next chapter that it's possible, and sometimes easy.)

Here are some creative and successful Lean and Green tactics to spark your imagination about improvements at *your* organization:

Hey—don't throw that away! Before 1994, any employee caught taking wood from one of Texas Instruments' dumpsters was fined. This policy existed because management was afraid of liability from accidents or injury. In 1994 management changed the policy: Now anyone can raid the dumpster of broken pallets or crates and use the wood to build sheds in their backyards or for other purposes. Not only is this a perk for employees, but it is a way of recycling and reduces TI's disposal costs.

> **Inspired by Model Trains?**
> While walking down a corridor in LSI Logic's flagship facility in Oregon, I looked up and saw what looked like a model train on a track in a rectangular glass tube affixed to the ceiling. It was a cart transporting semiconductor wafers (disks from which individual semiconductor chips are sliced; also see Glossary) in a miniature clean-room environment. An employee had realized that the eight-inch wafers did not need a whole people-sized room to move from one point to another, so why not use a model-train-sized "room"? The train — which rounds the corner to go inside, out of, and around the clean room — is a unique design that saves energy and reduces costs by eliminating the need for a full-sized clean room just for the transport of wafers.

What step comes before this one? One way to come up with creative solutions to pollution or waste problems is to ask yourself, "What step comes *before* this one?" Nirmal Singh at ITT Cannon provides an example (of course, some of the most creative ideas seem obvious only *after* they've been discovered): "We'd rather change the process such that we don't need to use any chemical whose impact we are not certain of. For example, we used to use a cleaning process after production employees handled a part—to remove fingerprints. We realized that we could have the workers wear gloves so that no fingerprints occur and that cleaning step can be eliminated!"

Why can't we do this for free? As Harry Reid at Agilent Technologies explains, "An engineer named Werner Gauss in the Boeblingen, Germany, site had an idea for cooling buildings for free. Werner explained it to me and I explained it to our building program development manager, who worked with consultants to adapt it to several European sites. Werner sits on the Boeblingen sustainability group—and this idea came out of his own environmental conviction." (More about Agilent's "free" cooling system is in Chapter 2.)

Steal an idea from elsewhere in your organization "Stealing" Lean and Green ideas is encouraged by most of the 20 organizations I studied. Steve Dolan at Compaq says, "Business units are encouraged to steal ideas for environmental programs from other business units."

Exchange green ideas with competitors Some of the Lean and Green companies' ideas came from other companies. Bob Barrett at ITT Gilfillan reports that at conferences environmental managers from Hughes and other military/aerospace companies network and talk with each other informally: "At the U.S. Navy's conference at China Lake last year, a Hughes employee expressed interest in a corrosion-resistant paint process I developed, and I shared it with him. People are willing to talk."

Skip over that polluting, time-consuming process Michel Compérat at Thomson Multimedia explained to me that television cabinets normally are painted to produce a smooth finish on the set. Thomson first minimized the caustic painting process by using organic solvents, then turned to even less environmentally intrusive water-based solvents. But then the company designed some television sets whose cabinets are no longer painted at all! Thomson Multimedia has invested in the plastic-molding process to create high-quality cabinets that are so smooth that paint is not needed for cosmetic reasons. Compérat says, "We're using just half the paint now that we did three years ago." He reports that the new plastic-molding equipment was expensive but explains that his company's paint-processing equipment, systems for capturing air emissions, treatment of water and waste, and the paint itself were all even more expensive. Also, the new molding process requires less plastic material. "So," he concludes, "we have less cost, less impact on water and air, and less waste."

I asked Compérat where the idea to invest in the plastic-molding process originated. "This was the idea of several people," he said, "especially Thomson Multimedia's mechanical development group. Initially the idea was mainly for quality improvement. But we are focusing more and more on manufacturing costs reduction and on the environment benefits also." He was proud to tell me that Thomson Multimedia's small TV assembly plant in Zyrardow, Poland, which was opened in 1998, has never used paint.

Wanted: Radical Notions

When questioning wasteful practices and designing Lean and Green steps to benefit profit and planet, let your creativity take you to places previously uncharted. Some of today's commonplace products and ways of producing them were once radical ideas. I asked some of the Lean and Green contacts, "What would your company really have to do, even if it's a radical notion, to contribute to the repair of the planet's ecosystems?" Here are my favorite responses:

▶ Tim Yeakley, chemical optimization project manager at Texas Instruments, says "Make semiconductors out of air and water. Use supercritical water, whose by-product is water."

▶ LSI Logic's Linda Gee thinks like Tim about making semiconductor chips radically differently for the least impact on the environment: "Perhaps we can use only baking soda, water, and sand to produce semiconductors, or use living brain cells for chips." She adds an idea that would not only reduce impact but also *repair* the planet: "We can perhaps make chips that can help speed up environmental remediation projects."

▶ The "radical notion" of Walt Rosenberg at Compaq is "to use no shipment packaging at all—packaging products using air. The ultimate would be when there's a computer on a chip that does not require fans and larger enclosures. Instead of disk drives and diskettes, we'll each have a flashcard we carry with us. Instead of using computer display screens, we'll wear glasses for individual viewing. Or we'll share one flat-panel computer display in each room; the screen saver will resemble a Rembrandt, so it looks like a painting. We'll have hand-held units that plug into computers."

▶ Frank O'Rourke at Celestica says, "The high-tech industry as a whole needs to be more prepared for radical changes (like CFC removal) than ever before. People are getting used to change, and it's getting more competitive." He suggests as a possible environmental solution in his industry bioelectronic devices and processes, even at the cellular level. Today this sounds radical, but tomorrow . . .

I encourage you to continuously think of ideas that will make products smaller, lighter, use fewer materials, and cost less.

And if you run out of creative juice, take a tip from Agilent's Martin Izatt: "To tell the honest truth, I've run out of ideas for conserving significantly more utilities. That's one reason I'm taking a new function (space planning and managing the engineering group, and keeping tabs on the construction of the new building), and passing along the utilities function to others who can look at these issues freshly."

MAKING IT EASY

Help Your Company Be Lean and Green
by Letting Your Creativity Soar

1. This week, notice and question the purchases made by your organization. Which items arrive in excess packaging that you just have to throw away or recycle? Could the packaging be removed or modified so that it serves a double purpose? Send an e-mail to the supplier addressed to the environment, health, and safety manager, describing your idea. In the subject field, enter "Lean and Green idea for your product."

2. Ask your friends who work for other organizations how they reduce waste or avoid polluting processes. Get the facts and suggest those ideas to your management. Make them aware of the nonproprietary Lean and Green steps *your* organization has taken.

3. Suggest to your manager a "radical" environmental goal, such as Werner Gauss's idea to cool the Agilent Technologies building "for free." Stress the money-saving aspect of the idea.

4. During breaks and lunch this month, tell your colleagues about some of the Lean and Green ideas in this chapter that impressed you most. You'll inspire others to think creatively.

One creative idea for environmental and cost savings at your organization can make more difference than a lifetime of an individual family's recycling efforts at home.

Chapter 2

Gain Lean and Green Endorsement Using Business Language

We want to improve quality of life by means of our products and services. The usual business approach for quality of life is short term—generating profit in the year and earning annual bonuses. From a long-term perspective, however, quality of life means going for a sustainable society. It's important to translate sustainability into pragmatic business achievements over the years, such as defining a waste reduction goal of 28 percent that yields savings of 250 million Dutch guilders and designing green products that win greater market share.

—Henk de Bruin, manager,
Corporate Environmental and Energy Office, Philips

I HOPE that Chapter 1 inspired you to create several ideas for exchanging polluting, wasteful practices for cost-reducing ones. The second Lean and Green step is to *gain endorsement* for Lean and Green ideas using business language. Introduce your environmental points with profit in mind—starting with strategies that yield the highest rewards to profit and planet.

Before you started reading this book, you may already have been convinced that your organization could be kinder to the environment and benefit from the associated cost savings or new sources of revenue. But if it seems to you that getting management's approval for your Lean and Green ideas is like pushing a boulder up a steep hill, this chapter is especially for you. Here I offer practical approaches to convincing management to be leaner by being greener. I also tell you how to avoid discouraging your organization from being Lean and Green: you'll find out which tactics are uninspiring and convince few managers to change their positions.

Tie Your Heartfelt Environmental Message to Profitable Returns

If you are passionate about preserving the environment and yet you see your and other organizations as part of the problem, you may want to *demand change now*. If you want an immediate stop to anything your organization is doing to pollute air and water, fill in beautiful bodies of water with ugly landfill, use natural resources wastefully, and send into the atmosphere gasses that foster global warming, your first instinct is probably to pitch to your management a message of change that goes to the heart of global survival. I, too, want organizations to adopt greener practices as quickly as possible. But hold on a moment before you get an audience with management.

When you interlace your environmental points with ideas for practical, profitable gain for the organization, you significantly increase the chance that your management will approve changes—and soon. Let me say this more strongly. If you *don't* lead your environmental idea with a sound business case—skipping this step either out of passion or from not yet knowing how to speak business language—you could actually become a Lean and Green *detractor*. A detractor turns management against environmental ideas and delays or even cancels proactive environmental steps.

For just a moment, consider the perspective of an organization like Apple Computer. There is no reason for Apple to do business, say my contacts there, *only* to "do good." All pro-environmental decisions made by the company to date have been good business decisions, especially to get Apple through its ups and downs in the market. From a product perspective, the business case rules.

The key business principle is profit. Ask yourself these questions:

▶ Will the environmental changes I want the organization to make reduce costs much more than the total cost of the change?

▶ Is the change highly likely to increase sales by more than the cost of the change?

▶ Will the change prevent an environmental mistake that would have eroded the company's market share (reducing sales and profit), owing to fines, cleanup, and negative publicity?

The good news is that nearly every idea to reduce waste, curb pollution, and use resources more efficiently yields a yes to one or all three of these questions. And it is this yes that you can feature when presenting your ideas to management.

Speak Business Language

You might see business language as being cold or elusive. But speak the language anyway. No one drives this point harder than Walt Rosenberg at Compaq. He says about making environmental improvements with the organization, "This isn't a touchy-feely area. It's good for business. We are not telling our senior vice presidents that environmental steps are good for the world, the right thing to do for our grandchildren. . . ." Walt rolls his eyes. "I'd get thrown out. They would respond with, 'You're right, it's nice. Bye-bye.'"

Walt began working in the environmental arena 20 years ago, mainly because he was interested in the technology and realized there could be a business benefit: "It's always been about business benefit. It just was not communicated effectively." Walt believes that third-party environmental groups' message to "save the world" is not the way to get the attention of individuals and corporations. Businesspeople may agree that the environmental benefits are desirable, but unless they also see the business benefit they won't take action, he says. Also, Walt observes that when third-party environmental organizations call attention to only one environmental concern, businesspeople rarely see how that issue applies to them or their corporations.

Most of Compaq's senior environmental personnel have master's degrees in business or something else and easily talk "business language." Walt Rosenberg says, "Because Compaq uses these senior managers to conduct the environmental audits and to recommend ways to enhance the managers' business position, some senior VPs report that the environmental audits are the best, most valuable audits they've experienced at Compaq."

How to Make a Business Case for Becoming Lean and Green

Don't worry, you don't need an MBA to make a strong Lean and Green business case. Just point out where non-green practices either increase expenses or hinder sales. Go ahead and make a strong case to management that environmentally detrimental practices are likely to increase costs and decrease revenues. Do some homework up front. You can present examples from this book about the cost of irresponsible or inadequate environmental policies, or better yet, show probable and realistic costs in your own operation.

If you wanted to persuade IBM to adopt your environmental idea, for example, you would tie the idea to a quantifiable return on investment. Environmental investments—just like other investments—must earn a standard return; this is the amount of money that taking a particular action (such as buying new equipment) earns or saves a company. According to Edan Dionne, manager of corporate environmental affairs at IBM, a manager compares a prospective new project's performance objectives with other options that could foster the company's competitiveness: "In general, individual capital investment decisions must jump the company's financial hurdle rate [return on investment requirement] to be considered."

Find out what payback hurdles *your* organization requires you to jump (by asking your controller, for example), and determine how your Lean and Green idea measures up. Because green practices so often *do* equal lean business results, chances are you will be able to show financial gain. For inspiration, see how employees at these Lean and Green organizations proved the financial benefit of their environmental ideas:

▶ Celestica requires a 20 percent annual return on investment and also considers "net present value" (see Glossary). Martin Oseni, who helps take care of the company's facilities, wanted Celestica to purchase a rooftop ice storage system that makes ice during the usually chilly Toronto nights and cools the building during the day as the ice melts—saving energy and money. Martin's proposal, which calculated the projected savings in kilowatts, convinced management that Celestica's required return on investment would be met. In practice, the project easily cleared the financial hurdle saving the company $175,000 each year.

▶ One of Kyocera's manufacturing facilities in Japan has a project for wastewater recycling whose capital investment was paid off in only six months. Again, the Green project exceeded Kyocera's required return on investments.

▶ Agilent's plant management in Scotland wants equipment—whether for production or environmental improvement—to produce a minimum payback of 18 percent annually. Martin Izatt and his team developed, based on an idea originating at the company's Boeblingen, Germany, facility (by an engineer named Werner Gauss), a free cooling system, which creatively reduces electricity and replaced a system that used ozone-depleting CFC chemicals. The system runs as if two car radiators are placed back to back, transferring heat from one to the other. Izatt explains: "We run a loop from the site through one 'radiator' and the other 'radiator' is connected to the cooler. There, the heat evaporates off a large shower." The free cooling system cost about £45,000 and saves £8,000 each year in electricity, which meets the annual 18 percent payback requirement.

▶ Nirmal Singh at ITT Cannon says that the way to prove return on investment is the same for environmental projects as for any other kind of project: show the payback. For example, Cannon installed equipment to recycle oil and water on-site, eliminating the need to send the material to recycling facilities via transportation that is expensive and risks spillage. To justify purchasing the equipment, Cannon measured the projected reduction in water usage and other cost savings: the payback.

Focus First on the Biggest Lean and Green Winners If you're like me, you want to make the biggest difference to the health of the planet and its occupants as quickly as possible. Fortunately, big environmental gains tend to translate into big profits for organizations. So, focus first on those environmental ideas that have a larger positive effect on both the environment and your organization's finances. You'll find that your management will approve environmental purchases more readily when the degree of improvement is greater. When Apple was recycling 50 percent of incoming materials and employees told management that a vertical bailer would increase recycling to 80 percent, approval was no problem. But as Facilities Manager Bill Brunson says, "If now we requested a horizontal bailer so that we could increase recycling 1 percentage point (from 97.3 percent to 98.3 percent), it would be harder to sell."

Emphasize Reduced Risk to the Company What do you do if your environmental idea does not meet your organization's financial requirements? Nirmal at ITT Cannon told me, "Some of our environmental purchases will not produce a strong return on investment, but do eliminate carcinogens—it's the right thing to do." Fortunately for Nirmal and several of the other Lean and Green champions, some organizations' managements accept the idea that not all environmental projects need to be highly profitable. Alan Leibowitz at ITT Corporation's headquarters says that environmental projects often have lower payback hurdles to jump, "since we have more than a profit incentive to make the improvement. When we submit the project it has a code for 'mandatory.' If ITT gets payback within two years, the employees involved get bonuses; it's looked at as a side benefit."

So, go for the profit point first, and if the financial return is not as strong as that on another type of investment and won't make the company more productive, stress that the environmental project will reduce the organization's risk of getting fined and losing customers' good will. If you can't find *any* compelling argument for the cost savings of an environmental investment, you can point to Intel as an example of a highly profitable company that pays no attention to return. Intel's environmental group asked Intel's senior managers what investment return they expected on environmental expenditures. According to Environmental Manager Tim Mohin, the VP of engineering said, "I don't really look at that for environmental projects—if the environmental group thinks it's needed and it's the right thing to do, we just do it." Generally, Intel accepts that environmental projects return half as much as other projects. Even so, Intel's Dave Stangis says, "We spend lots of money on environmental projects on which we do not expect to receive economic benefits. From some of these projects, however, we see—years later—that there *were* economic benefits."

Avoid Being a Lean and Green Detractor

Employees and managers inside the workplace and environmentalists outside the workplace can either facilitate or detract from a company's Lean and Green success. Ways to detract include intimidating employees who have environmental suggestions, failing to link environmental improvements with cost savings or revenue generation, using tactics to embarrass the company, making inflammatory remarks or inciting violence, and being shortsighted by reducing waste in one area while increasing pollution in another. Be wary of making these mistakes—even when your heart is in the right place.

Using Inflammatory Tactics Some tactics used to pressure management to implement an environmental practice are dramatic and garner wide attention but in the end are not effective. They may release the pressure valve for people who think business should do more to protect the environment but not actually make a positive difference for the environment. Do you see yourself or others on the following list?

▶ A detractor issues a boycott without checking facts or talking with management. Boycotts can be effective ways to get management to do the right thing. They also can be ineffective and unnecessarily disruptive for consumers if based on incorrect "facts" and ignorance about management's position. What, if anything, is management doing to address the situation? If they're ignoring it, first make a solid business case using the tactics described in this book. Only as a last resort call an appropriate boycott.

▶ A detractor is political for his or her own benefit. Making a splash in the press raises the public's awareness of a company's environmental practices, but also puts the critic in the spotlight. Some corporate managers who receive calls and visits from outside groups wonder whether those groups are truly trying to benefit the environment or whether they're more interested in self-promotion. Sometimes one political group competes against another by using a third-party organization as a pawn. For greater effectiveness where the environment is concerned, work with management as pragmatically as you can, and cooperate with other groups who also want to benefit the environment.

▶ A detractor may make inflammatory remarks or even commit violent acts. Some people choose this path out of a sense of self-righteousness or outrage. But those who do so lose credibility and risk being arrested or sued.

Doing More Harm Than Good "Environmental efficiency and accountability are key for any company to be competitive," says Tadahiko Nozaki, general manager of NEC's Semiconductor Environmental Management Promotion Center. In keeping with this philosophy, some of NEC's semiconductor facilities have reached the goal of zero emissions. "Yet some of what they are doing may not be environmentally efficient for other facilities," says Nozaki; "for example, transporting industrial wastes to producers of particular products that are located far away from the NEC facility is not environmentally efficient." My contacts at NEC stress that a company has to be flexible. Just because one chemical element is considered safe today, does not mean it won't be declared hazardous tomorrow. So a company has to monitor all those developments and be aware of what is going on.

Recommending Shortsighted Solutions Nirmal Singh at ITT Cannon gives an example of how good environmental intentions without the proper homework can backfire for environment, health, and business: "When I started at Cannon, we used 22 vapor degreasers using CFCs [chemicals that contribute to ozone thinning]. The challenge was to find a replacement for ozone-depleting chemicals that doesn't cause smog and isn't flammable or carcinogenic. The chemical HCFC was recommended; I was cautious—let's first see if it causes cancer. Now studies show it causes tumors in rats. Some HCFCs will be banned." So Singh formed a team and discovered they could replace CFCs with water-based cleaners in some cleaning stages. By avoiding a shortsighted solution that turned out to be carcinogenic, Singh says, "We shot directly for the water solution and fought ourselves and the status quo tooth and nail to get all the way there." Cannon eliminated storage tanks of solvents and 22 CFC solvents by switching to five water-based cleaners.

Avoid taking steps that will reduce your chances of convincing the corporation to do the right thing environmentally. I want to live on a planet with clean air and clean water, and I'm counting on you to present your environmental ideas to organizations in the most effective way possible—linking them to profitable business results. I hope this chapter has given you plenty of examples for making a strong business case. Here's one more tactic before I end the chapter.

Appeal to the Competitive Spirit

It's safe to say that most managers are motivated to compete with peer organizations, win more market share, get positive publicity, and enjoy greater financial rewards. Henk de Bruin gives an example of competition that motivated Philips to make some big environmental moves. A big company like Philips, with 250,000 employees, doesn't change direction quickly. So early in the 1990s de Bruin started to appeal to employees' and management's competitiveness. That same year, he conducted a study of competitors' environmental practices and consumer preferences, then told the Board of Management, "We can go further," and started the EcoVision program. EcoVision is a Web-based tool that makes sure all Philips operations are meeting the company's environmental improvement goals. Today, Philips gives EcoVision awards to its outstanding managers and to green products that give Philips a competitive advantage. And in 1998 Philips earned the World Environment Center's Gold Medal Award for International Corporate Environmental Achievement. At *your* organization, try appealing to your managers' competitive spirit!

MAKING IT EASY

Build Strong Business Cases for Lean and Green Success

1. Familiarize yourself with your organization's profit and loss statements as well as with management's top goals. It helps to speak management's language when making your Lean and Green case.

2. Increase your comfort level with business concepts such as profit and loss, return on investment, and risk management. I recommend two books: *Profit Building: Cutting Costs without Cutting People* by Perry J. Ludy (Berrett-Koehler Publishers) and *Finance and Accounting for Nonfinancial Managers*, by William G. Droms (Perseus Press). If you're at ease with business concepts, your business case for environmental improvement will be strong and your passion for the idea will help your case.

3. Avoid alienating management from your environmental message. First, be clear about *your* motivations. Is your aim to solve an environmental problem for the long run? Or are you looking to harm an organization out of bitterness or shortsightedness? (I assume that if you are reading this book you are in the former category!)

4. Don't be afraid to blow the whistle, point out threats to profit, and aim for radical environmental improvement — *as long as your points are good for business.*

5. Choose your battles carefully. Is the environmental goal you have in mind reachable? Will it make a more significant improvement to the environment, given the cost and effort, than other environmental goals at the organization? Are you considering long-term benefit over short-term flash?

6. In convincing management of your environmental ideas, try some of this chapter's proven ways to sell environmental ideas to management — keeping in mind their goals and style.

You can make your heartfelt points in your organization about the environment in good-for-business terms. You'll see swifter and more complete approval of these ideas thanks to your strategy when presenting them.

Chapter 3

Collaborate to Achieve Lean and Green Goals

> The dream and the beliefs are at the corporate level and they
> trickle down to us. Nothing could be effective if we didn't all
> believe in the same thing.
>
> —Barney Little, general manager, Horizon Organic Dairy

ACHIEVING Lean and Green goals is not a lonely process. In this chapter, get an overview of the third Lean and Green step: Collaborate throughout the organization to meet Lean and Green goals. If you can, first get your organization's senior leaders to support the Lean and Green way of improving the company's profitability while helping to restore natural resources for the coming generations. Then motivate people throughout your organization to create and implement Lean and Green solutions.

Start with Green Direction from the Top

Your organization will move faster toward becoming Lean and Green if you first obtain buy-in at the top. Water flows most easily downhill, and so do organization-wide directives. Once your leaders endorse the goal of using fewer resources, which will reduce costs and preserve the health of the planet, employees will follow suit—not only because they hold the planet dear, but also because they want to do well in their jobs.

Compaq Computer's director of corporate environmental affairs, Walt Rosenberg, stresses the importance of environmental commitment from the top: "If you don't have commitment from top management first—to measure it, financially support it, and talk it—the rest is a waste of time."

When top managers are exposed to business-savvy reasons to be committed to the environment organizationally, their environmental awareness trickles down to division managers, their management teams, and individual employees. Len Rosen, ITT Gilfillan's general manager in the 1980s, was inspired by an ITT corporate meeting on the environment. Rosen told his team back at Gilfillan, "We are going to take a proactive stance on how we treat chemical use in our operations." After Rosen read up on the effects of water and soil contamination, he told his employees to take out a perfectly good gas storage tank. He anticipated that the tank *could* leak and wanted "sleep insurance." See how swiftly organizations take environmental action when their leaders are behind it?

Here's another example of the power of a high-level environmental directive. When Mac Booth was CEO at Polaroid, according to Senior Engineer of Health, Safety, and Environment Ian McKeown, Booth noticed that several of his managers were environmentally active. Shortly after that, Booth announced at the end of a stockholders' meeting that the company would be introducing an environmental challenge to reduce "all waste by 50 percent in a five-year period." He called it the "50 in 5 Program." McKeown says, "Mac kick-started Polaroid into making radical improvements to the company's environmental performance."

You might say at this point, "I don't even know what my

organization's leaders think about the environment, and if I had to guess I'd say they don't think much about it, compared to quarterly profits." You might be right. In fact, fewer than half of the founders or leaders of the Lean and Green organizations featured in this book started out with strong environmental goals.

In those cases, people within the organizations who believed in the Lean and Green promise took the message to the top. They made a convincing argument there and saw that the message trickled down throughout the organization.

"Right," you may say nervously, "but how can *I* tell my organization's leaders what to do?" Remember from Chapter 2 that it's best to lead Lean and Green suggestions with a strong business case. Point out to management what you see as wasteful practices in the organization that can be improved for financial benefit and will make the organization a better corporate citizen as well. Now you're talking their language and are apt to get swift attention.

When the top of your organization supports Lean and Green goals, you will have a much easier time getting funding for projects that both reduce cost and improve the environment. Linda Gee at LSI Logic says that because the company's vice president believes environmental projects can reduce solvent emissions those projects get priority. When the VP approved the purchase of LSI's solvent-recycling equipment, his understanding of the Lean and Green promise produced results: LSI achieved a return on its investment in less than one year.

Collaborate on Lean and Green Goals throughout the Organization

Once the top of the organization has endorsed changes for profit and planet, it's time to inspire people throughout the organization to implement Lean and Green steps already developed and think of new Lean and Green ideas.

Effective organizational change results from true collaboration on the part of employees and their managers. After all, managers may know what steps need to be taken, but they rarely can take them all by themselves. Also, managers will not think of some changes that can make significant improvements to profit and planet. Few managers know their employees' jobs better than the employees actually doing those jobs every day.

At a Louisiana-Pacific wood-products mill in eastern Oregon, I interviewed several mill workers who told me that they are encouraged to give management environmental suggestions and report any concerns they have. These workers are much closer to the day-to-day uses of resources and are more likely than management to see where improvements can be made.

Most of the Lean and Green companies I've studied have become Lean and Green through "decentralized" implementation. This means that instead of managers giving employees strict and detailed instructions for making their jobs more profitable with less negative impact on the environment, managers give overall direction but then count on employees to know how best to implement the improvements.

British Aerospace's environmental organization is decentralized. Instead of receiving specific instructions from Environmental Advisor Danny Martland, each business unit creates its own environmental plan. Martland helps the business units assess environmental risk and plays the role of strategist and facilitator, as the title environmental advisor (which he thought of) suggests. He says, "I'm skeptical about environmental organizations with lots of people working for them. Maybe a large, centralized organization is better for a technical approach. But we use a people approach. It may take longer, but it creates bigger moves."

The company's Samlesbury, England, site employs 4,500 people. Martland envisions an ultimately decentralized environmental organization, achieved through training all employees and empowering them to take environmental steps both during and after work: "Our long-term objective is to have 4,500 'environmental managers.' It's a good motivational strategy. Employees realize that the company really cares about the environment, as evidenced by letting them take time off from work for environmental action at home or in the community." Martland believes in enlisting everyone in the search for environmental solutions, not only technical and environmental specialists: "Technical people can be boring, and the technical approach doesn't always communicate as well as focusing on the people does. So instead, get everyone on board—including the technical people who are designing the aircraft. I see that most of the work is initiated through the people side."

The same decentralized strategy—empowering employees to take local environmental action—is applied at Compaq. "We believe in the decentralized model," says Walt Rosenberg at Compaq, "because people are closer to the business than they otherwise would be. We want the environment, health, and safety person not to be seen as 'the EH&S person' but as a key business thinker."

The decentralized approach to meeting the worldwide goals works well because resources, business cultures, and environmental regulations vary from region to region. Why not let each region decide best how to meet environmental goals? Ian McKeown of Polaroid says, "Our culture here in Scotland is somewhat different from that of Polaroid in the U.S. Plus, Europe's environmental laws are different."

Motivating All Employees to Work the Lean and Green Way

The two most effective ways I've seen to encourage all employees to collaborate in "Leaning and Greening" their organizations are (1) to make Lean and Green goals part of employees' standard performance expectations, and (2) to create employee incentives on top of that.

Set Expectations for Employee Performance I believe that most people want to perform well, please their management, and feel good about their accomplishments. So to motivate most employees one has to make it clear what is expected of them. Compaq does this well with Lean and Green in mind.

Compaq's executives and their employees are measured on meeting their business-plan objectives—covering quality, production, the environment, and other factors. Each factor is weighted differently: at one site, meeting environmental goals within the business plan may account for 20 percent of an employee's bonus; at another site it may account for 10 percent. "The weight depends on challenges faced in each site and the local executive's leanings," says Walt Rosenberg. "It's good that we can get environmental objectives into the bonus plan; in fact, these goals are treated no differently from any other quality factor." In Brazil, for example, 25 percent of the top executives' bonus is based on their meeting environmental, health, safety, and security objectives.

Reward Accomplishments That Exceed Expectations Kids in school perk up when they get a chance to earn extra credit. So do employees when offered special recognition or a monetary bonus for benefiting the organization and the environment. See which of these ideas, taken from around the world, best match the culture of your organization:

▶ Dawne Schomer of Texas Instruments' Corporate Environmental, Safety, and Health group in Texas says that giving employees incentives to meet environmental goals and consulting with them during site reviews works better than "policing" them. TI is one of the many Lean and Green organizations that measures employees' success in implementing environmental programs, such as water reuse and chemical optimization, by using established bonus programs based on employees' annual performance plans.

▶ An LSI Logic employee in the company's German design center named its green team "HERO"—Helping the Environment with Rethinking Operations. The environmental department gives awards such as T-shirts and dinner for two to employees with good ideas.

▶ Kyocera, in Japan, has developed an Enlightenment Program to keep employees informed about environmental issues. The program includes an employee newsletter and Environmental Awareness Month (June) during which environmental events are held. Kyocera does not plan to stop at the workplace. The company is thinking about extending its environmental protection activities to employees' households, perhaps by publishing a newsletter that describes how to recycle and otherwise protect the environment, and illustrating it with examples. Kyocera would consider giving its environmental award to employees who take environmental action in their personal lives.

▶ Most people think of Apple Computer, based in California, as having a fun culture. Incentives for Sacramento employees to exceed the site's 95 percent recycling rate are right in line with this culture. The money earned from recycling funds parties, ice cream gatherings, and recognition awards—including certificates that can be redeemed at the on-site company store for T-shirts and other items. "We tell them, 'Recycling dollars paid for this,'" says Apple's Bill Brunson, who announced Apple's 97.3 percent recycling achievement.

▶ Philips, based in the Netherlands, has an employee EcoVision award for which applications are judged by an international jury. Philips's president or vice president flies in for the awards ceremony. Two monetary awards are given: one for the most ecologically friendly product and the other for the best ambassador of ecological practice. One winning idea in the product category was for a resource-efficient monitor; an environmental coordinator in Mexico won for the ambassador category. Most winners donate the money to charitable causes—including those that are environmentally focused.

Whether an organization makes Lean and Green goals part of employees' jobs or offers incentives to motivate employees to take profitable, environmental steps, it doesn't need to create a new system for giving and rewarding performance. An organization can communicate Lean and Green performance expectations and incentives using existing job descriptions and performance reviews.

Hold Employees Responsible for Effecting Positive Change The example from Celestica that follows offers a good summary of how environmental direction from top management can lead to creativity and implementation by employees—and to measurable results.

Celestica's environmental managers from several dozen sites around the world meet semiannually to receive Celestica's corporate instructions on chemical management programs and environmental policy. Frank O'Rourke, the EHS manager, explains that at these meetings the corporate environmental managers lay out the company's aspirations and some specific new programs they want implemented. Then they say, "How you do it is up to you; you know your own business. But we'll audit your site to be sure you'll have these programs in place." This approach is in keeping with Celestica's value system, says O'Rourke, which bases decisions more on consensus than on strict hierarchy.

Create Lean and Green Synergies throughout the Organization

Once your top management understands that Green resource efficiency leads to Lean and healthy organizations, and employees are on board, your organization's Lean and Green practices will snowball when you share the best ideas. I like Intel's approach to getting the word out about environmentally sound and profitable ideas—quickly and worldwide.

Larry Borgman, Intel's director of environment, health, and safety, recommends that environmental planning at all organizations start with "visioning" by the corporate environmental managers and top management; their vision can then be distributed throughout the company. The structure Intel developed for efficiently disseminating environmental information to employees is called a matrix. It is a computer-based compendium of solutions to a wide variety of environmental issues submitted by employees around the world. Borgman says, "The matrix has day-to-day hands-on employees with environmental responsibility reporting to their most logical, direct local management chain. The managers feel they own [can manage directly] the environmental employees and the environmental employees have no doubt who their customer is. Yet they are not isolated—they tie to a matrix that's quite strong; they know they can come to their siblings in other locations and corporate management for help." The company culture encourages questioning and asking for help—even stealing ideas. According to Borgman, "We say, 'Steal with pride.' We promote the Great Steals we've had from other groups each week."

Ninety percent of Intel's environmental employees are in the field, and only 10 percent in corporate—but most of the corporate employees used to be in the field. "I try not to get deeply involved in the affairs of a site," says Borgman, "no more at the facility five miles from my office than in sites that are 1,000 miles away. I say, 'Look to the matrix for the answers—not to corporate.'" This solution has worked so well that nonenvironmental Intel groups want to see how the matrix works. Borgman believes that the matrix has been a key factor in keeping waste down, even as Intel's revenues quadrupled from 1992 to 1998. His mantra is, "Measure us by our results." He adds, "No senior manager in the company can disagree with this."

When Necessary, Collaborate *Outside* Your Organization

In Chapter 2, I warned against using inflammatory tactics that detract from Lean and Green progress. But that doesn't mean you shouldn't use key resources outside your organization if they will contribute to environmental improvements. Here are positive ways to use examples and advocates from outside your organization to garner immediate respect and action from management:

▶ **Cite negative case studies** After the oil tanker *Exxon Valdez* ran aground in Alaska, contaminating the shoreline and killing large numbers of birds and fish, Exxon's business dropped significantly. The truth is that environmental mistakes can have a negative impact on revenues. So go ahead—make a strong case to an organization's management that environmentally unfriendly practices may well harm their business by generating negative publicity and leading to reduced sales, just as has happened at other organizations.

▶ **Team up and sue** Bill Zehnder at ITT Gilfillan says the air in the Los Angeles area is worse than anywhere in the country: "An air pollution control district derives its funds from the health of the economy. The Los Angeles area experienced an economic downturn several years ago and the air district had to lay off staff, which meant that the South Coast Air Quality Management District [SCAQMD] couldn't monitor and control as much as before. Local environmental groups such as the Sierra Club and the Coalition for Clean Air got fed up and sued. They got orders from courts saying that government agencies, such as the SCAQMD, have to try harder."

▶ **Tell the media** When the media blow the whistle, business revenues can suffer for a long time, as the city of Santa Monica, California, found out. According to Dean Kubani, Santa Monica's sustainable city program director, "A significant portion of businesses here realize that their revenues are tied to the local environment; people come to the city for the beach. In the mid-1980s the national newspapers reported that Santa Monica Bay was polluted. No tourist would fly from Germany to Santa Monica to visit a polluted beach." The work by Kubani and other city employees to clean up the beach and other areas of the environment has been so exemplary that Kubani spends nearly half his time describing to other government organizations how Santa Monica turned its situation around. But even today that long-ago news story's effect on Santa Monica continues: The cab driver who drove me from Santa Monica to Los Angeles International Airport asked, after I told him I was visiting Santa Monica for a book on the environment I'm writing, "Is it safe to swim at the Santa Monica beach? Isn't there bacteria in the water?" That is the lasting effect of blowing the whistle, and it's entirely appropriate to blow the whistle in ways businesses understand.

MAKING IT EASY

Become a Lean and Green Organization through Collaboration Organization-Wide

1. Save time and frustration by taking the Lean and Green message first to the top of your organization. Steps to enhance profitability and the health of the planet are most effective when they are supported by top management.

2. "Decentralize" how Lean and Green goals are met. Let managers give direction, but then count on employees to figure out the best ways to make improvements. If people are told to execute policy in a prescribed way, you could miss out on the most creative and effective solutions by individual employees.

3. Make Lean and Green results part of each employee's performance expectations, and reward those who go beyond expectations with culturally appropriate recognition or prizes.

4. Share the best solutions with the rest of your organization. ("Stealing" is encouraged in this case.)

5. Audit the organization's progress to be sure Lean and Green practices are carried out and to find out in which areas employees need the most support.

6. When necessary, team up with people outside your organization to motivate organizations to become Lean and Green.

You've now created organization-wide collaboration in meeting Lean and Green goals, starting with buy-in at the top and empowering the people best able to make it happen!

Chapter 4
Track Progress for Environment and Profit

> The successful companies are those who can relate environmental changes to business performance. Upper management has to meet financial analysts' projections, as well as see the big picture—meeting quarterly goals five years from now.
>
> —Walt Rosenberg, director of
> corporate environmental affairs, Compaq

THE fourth of the Lean and Green steps measures and enforces all the progress you've made in the first three: Measure your organization's Lean and Green progress, and strive continuously to improve. See that the Lean and Green steps your organization is taking are truly healthful both for planet and for profit, and keep raising the bar.

Here are three good reasons you should track the environmental progress your organization is making, along with the money being saved or earned:

1. You'll see that you're on track to meeting your Lean and Green goals.

2. If you are off track, you'll have the insight necessary to get back on track.

3. You and your management, customers, shareholders, and community will know that your green efforts truly are contributing to a healthy, lean organization. As a result, you will have an easier time getting future Lean and Green ideas approved.

I really want you to take this step of measuring your Lean and Green results, whether you are fluent in accounting and love business ratios or are intimidated by databases, profit-and-loss tables, and comparison charts. Why? Because most of your managers are in the former category, and it's critical to demonstrate to them—with the data they respect—that environmental steps also make sense for the business's bottom line. I want you to be successful in conveying your Lean and Green recommendations.

Don't worry—this chapter tells you how to easily track cost savings from environmental improvements such as reducing utilities and reducing, reusing, and recycling materials. Here's one example: Apple Computer tracks cost savings from environmental steps on a product-unit level. Apple's Brian Rauschhuber says, "Our environmental program saves money, and we can attribute cost savings to it. How can you tell you're doing well unless you can measure it? It's not that time-consuming to analyze cost down to the product unit; we refer to reports sent by our vendors."

You can do *that*, right? Read on.

How Much Tracking Is Cost-Effective?

Lean and Green organizations Texas Instruments and Intel both manufacture semiconductors. Yet these two companies are at two opposite ends of a spectrum regarding *how much* environmental data to track. Shaunna Sowell, TI's VP and corporate staff manager for worldwide facilities, told me that her group sends to all

TI plants and every business manager worldwide a bar chart tracking environmental performance against the goals: "We are an engineering company; we are obsessive-compulsive about data." TI tracks the cost of environment, health, and safety issues per semiconductor pin (see Glossary). In contrast, Tim Mohin, environmental manager at Intel, responded to my question about tracking cost savings from environmental projects as follows: "We don't have enough precise data on money savings. Why? We're too damn busy. People are working 80-hour weeks." Interestingly, both companies' management teams use "cost savings" as their reason for being on their particular end of the spectrum.

British Aerospace is at the center of the spectrum. "You can fill the time of a disproportionate number of people by having them chase data," says Environmental Advisor Danny Martland, "or you can measure too little and fail to put over the business case for environmental programs, which influences senior management to support them. We take the middle road. We track data that's easy to get a hold of, such as waste and use of solvents. If there are no data, it's harder to point senior management to the benefits." Sometimes, though, the benefits of environmental programs may be on the public relations side only. Danny makes this point by asking rhetorically, "Why does our company get involved in numerous community environmental projects? You can't measure the benefits, and we wouldn't pursue these if we were only chasing statistics."

Dean Kubani, sustainable city program coordinator in Santa Monica, suggests formulating specific goals. When goals are vague—when they are just a direction—constituents can say, "Everything's great." But Kubani continues, "Specific targets create imperative and accountability. The city council and staff feel accountable and realize someone is going to ask questions if we don't meet our targets." For example, Santa Monica set an eight-year goal to convert 75 percent of its fleet to vehicles run on electricity or fuels other than gas and diesel. The city started out at 10 percent in year one and reached only 15 percent in year three. The Environmental and Public Works Management Department was able to announce that it would not reach its goal of 75 percent at that pace. That announcement motivated the city to look more closely at its fleet purchases and set up a program for fleet vehicle retirement in order to reach its goal. By year seven, 65 percent of the fleet was using electricity or alternative fuels. Another set of statistics tracking a specific goal caused quick action: "Bus ridership dropped in a five-year period," says Kubani. "This triggered concern by the city council, which led to the Transportation Department conducting interviews with 3,000 bus riders, revising routes, assigning different sized buses, and improving signage. Ridership rebounded and we have far surpassed our target."

What to Track

According to Ian McKeown at Polaroid, "If you can't measure it you can't manage it." So let your organization's environmental policy and goals inform *what* to track. To give you some ideas, here are some examples from the Lean and Green companies. Thomson Multimedia tracks the cost of materials used in its TVs and other consumer products, its compliance with environmental regulations, and its consumption of water, energy, and power— correlating the latter with global savings per year. The company saved $2.8 million by using one less kilowatt per employee hour worked in 1998 than in 1997.

LSI Logic tracks how much of the materials it purchases gets included in products, how much is emitted into the air or water, and how much gets wasted. Monthly energy consumption and hazardous waste are listed in environmental management reports.

Ian McKeown at Polaroid reports, "Our facilities people keep track of water and energy saved. We continuously are asked by corporate to reduce costs, such as by 5 percent. We ask ourselves, 'Is there any one thing we can do to reduce consumption?' We continually look at reducing our resources such as electricity, air, heating, and lighting. Most of the systems are computer controlled and we can get printouts on our costs, so it's easy for the division manager to see if costs are up or down."

Sony's top international priority is to fight global warming, so the company tracks energy consumption, fuel used to generate power, and carbon dioxide emissions according to its Environmental Action Plan. Every year, each business unit of Sony reports its environmental data and chemical use to Sony's Environmental Conservation Committee in Japan, which determines whether the Environmental Action Plan's objectives are being met. In Japan, the company reduced the waste disposed of per unit of sales by 30 percent in four years, to 54 percent of waste generated. Among the most effective measures were recycling sludge to make cement, making concentrates from waste alkaline substances, and devising ways to reuse packaging materials. Sony's goal for 2010 onward is not to dispose of any waste in landfills. Sony now is studying ways to quantify the environmental impact of its products themselves.

TI has been focusing on reducing the cost of goods sold (COGS) in order to compete well in cost per pin with competitors in Taiwan and Japan. "Three years ago we benchmarked with competitors and found that our product was more than 75 percent higher than best-in-class COGS," says Shaunna Sowell. "A key part of our three-year effort has been environmental business decisions on COGS per unit volume, including the cost of energy, water, gas, chemicals, and some consumables. In one year we reduced the cost of environmental, health, and safety issues per pin by 26 percent, which translated to $60 savings per wafer. Our goal was to save an additional $58 per wafer; and even when our plants are underutilized when the semiconductor business is down, we still reached the goal. In semiconductor assembly and test our goal is to save 33 cents per pin [an 18 percent improvement]; we'll probably make it."

Tools for Tracking an Organization's Environmental Impact

It's helpful to automate your organization's system for tracking environmental impact and related costs. Automation is not essential, however. Two of the 20 Lean and Green organizations still compile paper-printed environmental procedures, regulations, and results in binders on shelves, instead of on a widely-accessible electronic system.

Many companies use standard business software programs, such as Microsoft Word and Excel, for keeping track of environmental policies and their correlating money savings or new revenues. Others use specialized programs, like QMX (used by Celestica), that automatically notify people when an environmental procedure or audit is due. Frank O'Rourke at Celestica says, "If I ignore the note QMX sends me and fail to update an environmental procedure or audit, after a month my manager is notified; after another month *his* manager is notified."

Some Lean and Green companies have developed their own information technology tools for tracking environmental impact. For example, Texas Instruments developed the world's first electronic bulletin board, called TIOLR (pronounced *tylore* and standing for TI's Online Reporting System). Employees use TIOLR to track pounds of nonhazardous solid waste—per 150 millimeter wafer, per pin, and per region—as well as the cost of disposal. The system also tracks material that is recycled and shipped. Environmental tracking with the help of TIOLR has helped TI to reduce the overall cost per semiconductor wafer, which is a key profitability goal of the company.

EcoVision is a software system Philips developed to track wasted materials as a percentage of incoming materials and progress according to these environmental goals: reducing consumption of energy, water, and materials; lifecycle analysis and design for the environment; and reuse/recycling of materials. According to Henk de Bruin, "EcoVision is a monitoring system that resides on Philips's intranet; the system was activated in all sites within five months." For the lifecycle analysis and design elements, employees in each business group complete questionnaires about their product development plans. EcoVision then compiles the environmental impact data and generates graphs for the whole company; I saw one of these reports and was impressed with the quantitative data presented.

NEC licenses its internally developed Kankyo (environmental) Partners software to other companies preparing for ISO 14000 certification, auditing their environmental performance, and tracking regulations. This is yet another source of profitability through smart environmental ideas!

Accounting Methods for Tracking Environmental Costs and Profits

Key reasons for organizations to track environmental impact are to focus on areas that need the most improvement and to demonstrate to management that the finances of the company are better off for having taken green steps. *How* to measure the economic impact of these steps is a question being answered creatively by many Lean and Green organizations.

NEC Semiconductor Group is working with Japan's Ministry of International Trade and Industry (MITI) to introduce "environmental accounting" to its business. The new accounting procedures will keep track of the resources used to protect the environment and how much money has been saved or earned. In developing environmental accounting, NEC and MITI are answering these difficult questions:

▶ Should potential lost revenue be incorporated into the accounting system? For example, if your company is not green enough, your customers may purchase products and services from your competitors. But by being green, you prevent lost revenues.

▶ How best should an organization calculate cost savings from recycling materials in one year when, for example, it recycled 50 percent of its waste two years ago and an additional 25 percent last year? Should the savings for this year be calculated as just 25 percent?

▶ How can an organization measure environmental impact uniformly throughout its locations and divisions and track project-specific cost savings to promote accountability?

Michel Compérat at Thomson Multimedia developed an environmental index for tracking his company's European Environmental Coordinators performance against goals:

$$\frac{\text{Environmental item} \times 100}{\text{Total annual direct cost}} = \text{the Index}$$

Examples of an "environmental item" might include tons of waste or square meters of gas.

Tackling Environmental Auditing

So, now that you are convinced that to meet your organization's Lean and Green goals it's important to track environment progress and its effect on profitability, how can you be sure that the various groups and regions of your organization are implementing the environmental steps and doing so profitably? This is where the "environmental audit" comes in. It's a great tool for testing whether your organization is on track, or for learning how to get back on track.

Here I describe the audit system that Compaq Computer uses because it shows that even a large, global organization can encourage employees around the world to track and meet environmental goals. Kevin Famam, environmental program manager at Compaq, started auditing Compaq's worldwide environmental data by first compiling easy-to-measure costs, such as air emissions, waste produced, and energy consumed—relevant to all sites. Gradually, he got more and more sites to participate. When I asked Famam what he does if a site seems resistant to reporting the environmental data, he said "You talk them through it—it's not as onerous as you'd think. A lot of the information is already somewhere because Compaq is billed for it. I just pull it together."

Compaq's Audit Program Manual defines Compaq's audit process from beginning to end, including what the corporate auditors looked for at each Compaq site to minimize surprises. Walt Rosenberg says, "The audit is structured, detailed, and consistent from Scotland to Singapore so that the same measuring stick is used; this fosters fairness and drives Compaq to be consistent."

Who conducts these important environmental audits? At Compaq, audits are led by senior employees—90 percent are corporate staff. Rosenberg says, "We can't afford to use junior people for the audits when you think of what's at risk. To determine the business value of this particular standard, it takes senior people talking head to head with senior managers at the sites—going through their business plans and lots of sensitive documents. We have access to them all. In other contexts, auditors are junior folks who are not as respected and can be seen as a bother. We said, 'If we bring our best people to the table, both the environment and the value it brings to the company will be recognized and understood.'"

Consider that conducting environmental audits is well worth it, given the monetary gain to which the audits point and the fodder gained for future Lean and Green justifications. There's nothing like the results of an audit to bust the myth that environmental steps are expensive and detract from the company's profitability goals!

Measure Progress with the Long Term in Mind Even the best-intentioned people in organizations can detract from Lean and Green results by putting short-term gain ahead of long-term profit—profit both for business and for the environment. For example, some farms and dairies shy away from "going organic" because of the four-to-five-year transition period from conventional to organic. Barney Little, general manager of Horizon Organic Dairy, explains how his farm's long-term strategic view has paid off: "First we had to transition everything from conventional to organic, requiring different standards for the ground—no foreign inputs for three years, and livestock having to be fed organically for 12 months prior to milk production. This can be a four-year transition, during which you have to grow organically but sell at the lower conventional prices. These years are expensive and prohibitive for most people. We have a very profitable operation here, but to build up the herd it has taken years to recoup the costs—which we've nearly done." Little offers a complete picture of how longer-term thinking yields better profits for the organization and the environment; he refers to the requirements of being organic: "Nitrogen and other chemicals can perk up plants overnight, but compost helps the soil yield far greater benefit to plants in the longer term." He acknowledges that this longer view is "a huge commitment" on the part of a business.

Warning: With Excellent Tracking, You May Surpass Your Goals In a recent EcoVision report, Philips documented the company's progress according to its corporate goals for ISO 14000 certification and reduction of energy, water, waste, and releases (banned, hazardous, and relevant releases). Henk de Bruin says, "We've already surpassed some of our targets set for four years from now! We may increase our targets next year."

MAKING IT EASY

Track Your Environmental Progress

1. What should your organization track to hone your environmental action plans and make the best case for their profitability? Start by reviewing your organization's environmental policy and goals, and consider this chapter's examples from the Lean and Green organizations to get ideas.

2. You know yourself. If you are not good at tracking details, ask a colleague or assistant to set up the tracking system. Once it is well thought out and in place, you can see that your organization uses it so you can show off the proven cost savings of your environmental strategies.

3. Track as much as you can, but realize that some environmental impact cannot be tracked precisely. After giving me a table listing impressive measurable impacts of environmental savings on cost savings, Polaroid's Ian McKeown said, "So much of environmental impact is nonquantifiable. You can measure waste and energy usage, and the quantity and toxicity of material. It is difficult, however, to quantify impact on global warming, and the long-term liability of landfill."

Tracking your environmental progress allows you to prove to upper management that Lean and Green are one.

Part II
Real-Life Examples
of Putting Lean and Green into Practice

GET the strategies for action from this, the largest part of the book. "How to" descriptions and real-life examples will help you make the four Lean and Green steps happen at your workplace.

Read Part II straight through for great ideas about Lean and Green steps you can take in your organization, or use it as a reference when you write your environmental policy (Chapter 5), redesign processes and products (Chapter 9), or encourage suppliers to be greener (Chapter 13).

Whether your organization is a government entity, manufacturer, professional or personal service provider, school, transportation company, hospital, or any other type of workplace, I promise that you will relate to several of the more than 100 solutions to business or environmental issues in this part of the book.

Chapter 5

Make a Commitment
to Being Lean and Green

> We made our environmental goals big, because of their direct
> effect on reducing costs.
>
> —Paul Gowen, corporate environmental specialist,
> Texas Instruments

HOW many times have you heard, "Be careful what you ask for
. . . you might just get it"? I hope you've heard it many times
and have found—as I have—that it tends to be true. Developing
a two- to three-sentence policy about your organization's commitment to a healthy environment, and getting the policy approved by top management, goes a long way toward making
your policy a reality. A policy statement provides all employees
with a vision, declares your stance to customers and the community, and starts the process of real savings for the environment and your organization.

This chapter's nuts-and-bolts examples of how to develop and
begin implementing an environmental policy will help you make
Lean and Green steps 2 and 4 work at your organization: gain
endorsement using business language, and measure your Lean
and Green progress.

Tips on Writing an Effective Policy

If your organization's chief has not yet created an inspiring environmental policy to focus the entire organization on Lean and Green practices, you can start the process by drafting a policy, running the draft by stakeholders, then getting top management to endorse it. Yes—even if you don't have a master's degree in policy (I certainly don't), you can manage to draft a two- or three-page statement. Use these guidelines:

Keep It Short When I ask my clients how they meet organizational goals that depend on the actions of their employees, some show me noble but lengthy statements of company culture or principles. These long paragraphs are just too much for employees to grasp and put into action each day. It's best to keep your statement short so the message can be on the lips of every employee.

I find Thomson Multimedia's environmental policy, listed in the sidebar on page 77, to be punchy, action-oriented, and easy to read. My Lean and Green contact there is Dr. Michel Compérat, who directs environmental, health, and safety programs for the company in Europe. Compérat wanted his company's environmental charter to be short and use wording that emphasizes everyone's involvement in a continuous process of improvement. He says, "When charters include too much text, they are not efficient for employee awareness."

Texas Instruments' goal is "zero wasted resources and zero illnesses/injuries." Paul Gowen, corporate environmental specialist, explains that everyone at TI knows that "Zero Zero" refers to the company's environmental and safety goals. You can't make a policy much shorter than that.

Avoid Jargon Avoid using jargon or flowery words that convey too broad a promise or too weak a message. Sony's company policy disallows use of the phrases "kind to the Earth," "environmentally friendly," "environmentally correct," or other ambiguous slogans used in advertising and corporate communications.

Choose Simple and Precise Words Henk de Bruin at Philips says, "One of the challenges in working toward environmental sustainability is finding vocabulary that's easy to explain to management. I was a teacher in the old days, so I look for words that are easily understandable to others." Philips's publication *From Green to Gold*, which highlights the company's green products— from semiconductor chips to vacuum cleaners—lists five areas in which Philips enhances its products' environmental performance: hazardous substances, packaging, energy, recycling, and weight. "We use the word 'weight' to mean the amount of raw material used. Everyone understands that by reducing weight, more products fit in a truck and fewer resources are used." I agree that "weight" is more meaningful to most people than the business term "bill of materials."

Benchmark with Policies at Best-in-Class Organizations Harry Reid at Agilent Technologies and his team looked at best-in-class environmental reports from IBM, Ericsson, Nokia, Sony, Philips, and nearly 20 other high-tech companies as a basis for its own report. Using those companies' reports as a benchmark, Agilent based its own policy on a master's thesis on environmental reporting by Trevor Rae, Agilent's facilities operations manager in South Queensferry, Scotland.

Set High Goals for High Profit In your policy statement, aim high both for planet and profit. Three Lean and Green organizations— Louisiana-Pacific, Texas Instruments, and NEC—have set "zero emissions" or "zero waste" as goals. Liz Smith at LP says, "It is the foundation of what we call our 'journey to zero' that also includes a goal of zero employee injuries."

Shaunna Sowell traveled to every Texas Instruments site to talk to managers about TI's Zero Zero goal. Some people questioned it, asking "How can we ever reach zero wasted resources?" Sowell and her team helped people understand that although Texas Instruments might not achieve the data point of "zero," if the company could get closer to it than any competitor, Texas Instruments would win. "The only place you get profit from the manufacturing process is the product that goes out for sale," says Paul Gowen of TI. "Waste is the enemy of product profitability."

NEC's "Zero Waste" project is the company's most profitable program. Because 70 to 80 percent of all industrial wastes and other pollutants at NEC were produced by its semiconductor plants, the cost savings (leading to increased profit) in its semiconductor business is greatest in all of NEC. Now NEC is bolstering its Zero Waste activity by encouraging its communications-equipment divisions to take part.

Aim Policy at Early Processes for Maximum Cost Savings The earlier in your organization's processes that you incorporate environmental thinking, the greater the magnitude of improvements to the environment and your profitability will be. See how Philips, Intel, and Texas Instruments advocate this maxim.

Henk de Bruin says that Philips's initial environmental efforts were reactive, aimed at the "end of the pipe." Philips dealt only with the pollution caused by the manufacturing process, and did not look also at product design, reduction of resource use, and environmental sustainability. Philips's environmental activities were ahead of legislation, but not by much. "Then in 1991 for the first time," explains de Bruin, "Philips studied how to use the environment as an opportunity instead of a threat. We got signals from the outside world that environmental strategies could be an advantage. We made a two-year effort to get environmental *opportunity* on management's agenda."

Dave Stangis at Intel is following a similar course. "We're moving away from a *push* system, which employs negative reinforcement with erratic results, and toward a *pull* system, which fosters constant improvement. The push system is based on environmental-abatement technology—end-of-pipe solutions to meet regulations. The pull system is based on performance—impact on the environment." Starting thirty years ago, Intel's environmental management philosophy has evolved in the following stages:

1. **Push system:** Waste treatment

2. **Push system:** Waste minimization—purchasing fewer chemicals

3. **Pull system:** Pollution prevention

4. **Pull system:** Product and process design for the environment. For example, Intel is reducing emissions of volatile organic compounds as a percentage of silicon produced.

The final stage will be environmentally sustainable development, says Stangis.

Until 1994, Texas Instruments focused its environmental

efforts on complying with regulations worldwide. "We achieved good results with this focus," says Brenda Harrison, director of EHS services for TI in Dallas; "but we learned that reactive compliance with rapidly changing worldwide regulations didn't return to our bottom line. This end-of-pipe focus was costly, and our department was seen as the cost of doing business. So we looked at TI's future business goals: process efficiency and productivity, as measured around the country by performance metrics. We asked ourselves, 'Do environmental steps help efficiency and productivity?' and answered, 'Duh.' We created stretch goals of 100 percent productivity of our people and 100 percent process efficiency of our systems, including zero wasted resources."

How to Use Environmental Policy

Set your environmental policy centrally, but implement it locally. The strict hierarchical model for organizations is on its last dictatorial legs. Replacing this model is setting a vision (for environmental policy, for example), communicating it in an inspiring way, giving employees the tools and freedom to meet the organization's goals, and performing audits to ensure that the goals are met. Employees feel good about contributing to the overall goals while developing their own methods and creative solutions. The Lean and Green companies described in this book apply the newer organizational models, allowing individuals and small teams to meet environmental goals in their preferred manner.

Apple Computer's Bill Brunson is the senior person for environmental compliance at the Sacramento, California, site. He says, "Environmental action is not as effective in a hierarchical organization: I used to be in a valley screaming up to the folks on the cliff to hear me. It's frustrating and doesn't work well. So we have to integrate business and environmental action at all levels."

Enforce your organization's environmental policy by appealing to employees' values, educate them about how their actions and ideas affect both environment and profit, and offer rewards when Lean and Green goals are met. Linda Gee at LSI Logic says, "We give the policy to all employees during their orientation to educate them on what to do and what our priorities are—that compliance and pollution prevention are important. Plus, customers ask for it—we have a binder of more than 80 customer requests for information on our environmental management system, including requesting our environmental policy." LSI, like most of the Lean and Green companies, posts its environmental policy on its website.

Michel Compérat worked with Thomson Multimedia's communication department to have a graphic designer create small posters of the environmental policy, using the same color and graphics as in the company's annual report. The poster is available in several languages.

Part of inspiring employees to meet goals is training them so solidly that they can readily recite the goals and know how what they do every day fosters or hinders those goals. Paul Gowen at TI says,

Three Companies' Environmental Policies

Thomson Multimedia makes its operating principles short and clear. Sony emphasizes that the environment is a priority. NEC states a global vision for human potential on a clean planet.

THOMSON MULTIMEDIA

- ▸ Safeguard people
- ▸ Protect and preserve the environment
- ▸ Conserve resources
- ▸ Integrate Thomson's environment, health, and safety commitment into the strategic business planning and decision-making process
- ▸ Target communication and training as enablers

SONY CORPORATION

Recognizing that environmental protection is one of the most pressing issues facing mankind today, Sony incorporates a sound respect for nature in all of its business activities.

NEC

NEC Corporation will contribute to a sound environment and a livable society through technology that harmonizes with nature and production that is environmentally friendly. NEC's vision is a world where our natural environment is preserved, enabling all people of the world to pursue their full potential.

"Since the shift away from reactive compliance and toward the lofty goals of Zero Zero, terminology such as 'chemical optimization' is in everyday TI language. You don't hear people talking about abatement strategy or waste management strategies as much."

MAKING IT EASY

Write Your Environmental Policy

1. Choose the sample policies in this chapter — from Thomson, Sony, or NEC — that inspire *you* most in the context of your organization.

2. Tweak the words so the policy fits your organization.

3. Repeat step 2 until you really like the policy. Don't struggle with this — you will have a good draft after only 30 minutes of revisions.

4. Find five people at your organization who have fiscal responsibility, and five whom you think have an average or greater-than-average interest in a clean environment. Ask them if the policy would inspire them to make even one change in their job for Lean and Green benefit. Finalize the policy using their input.

5. Go to your organization's very top (the CEO, board president, or mayor), and say, "I've based this policy on those of some of the world's leading organizations, and several people at our organization said they'd be inspired to improve our profits through environmental steps if we adopt this. It's good for our organization's returns, morale, and public perception. Please consider it for our company."

6. When the top person agrees, send the policy to all employees, customers, constituents, suppliers, and the press.

You've taken the first step to creating a Lean and Green organization!

Chapter 6

Set Up an Environmental Management System

Use a holistic approach to environmental management that focuses on people. You have to keep people motivated; it helps when they see that our company is supporting them to get involved in the environment as much as they want. Then employees begin to say, "Our company really cares about the environment."

— Danny Martland, environmental advisor,
British Aerospace

HAS anyone ever accused you of saying the right words but not following through with action? I received this reprimand a few times during childhood, and it stung. If you haven't been on the receiving end of this accusation, you probably have made or heard accusations about leaders or organizations being "all talk and no action" when it comes to valuing customers, treating employees well, or *caring about the environment.*

An insincere commitment to the environment stings not only the leader or organization who uses the "nice" words, but also the environment itself. And the consequences of wasting resources and failing to reduce pollution can be irreparable: lost species of plants and animals and an ozone beyond repair. By the way, to achieve the *financial* benefits of the Lean and Green promise, an organization also has to follow through on environmental words with effective results.

The best way I've seen organizations translate their environmental words into actions is by creating and implementing an environmental management system. This chapter gives you ten suggestions for starting and actualizing a management system and lists common pitfalls to avoid—so that your organization can take the third and fourth Lean and Green steps: Collaborate throughout the organization to meet Lean and Green goals; measure your organization's Lean and Green progress, and strive continuously to improve.

What Is an Environmental Management System?

An environmental management system comprises environmental policies, how-to instructions, and accountability measures for continual improvement—a set of policies and activities that help your organization minimize harm to the planet *and* benefit from all the cost savings and revenue opportunities that Lean and Green organizations enjoy. A Lean and Green environmental management system, in the form of a booklet or a database, describes the cost savings or revenue gain of each activity so that management is reminded that not only the environment—but also the business—benefits.

A well-designed system informs people performing all of the organization's functions in all of its locations what Lean and Green goals to achieve, with guidelines for how to achieve them. It reduces the time and cost of searching for solutions that may already be working elsewhere in the organization, and the system minimizes expensive mistakes.

The Lean and Green role models I interviewed at Apple Computer in Sacramento are so pleased with the time-saving and cost-reducing features of their environmental management system that during my visit they showed off their database version of the system on a large projection screen. Of course, the system they created uses Apple equipment and software. Apple's Environmental Management System Manual and Environmental Impacts Database list all of the company's environmental documents and databases and describe the responsibilities of each group by function, rather than specifying what individual people should do. The system ranks Apple's environmental impact issues in order of importance; the highest priority is to reduce landfill.

Here's an example of how the system would help you save time and avoid negative environmental impact if you worked at Apple. Let's say you've arranged for a new contractor to work on the facility's air compressors and you'll need to tell the contractor what to do with the used oil. You would open the database from your computer, then sort the information by water discharge, electrical consumption, natural resource usage, or storm drainage. All of the applicable regulatory requirements will be listed, along with Apple's goals (which exceed requirements), and documents that tell what to do with the oil.

Ten Suggestions

I asked the 20 Lean and Green organizations for advice on creating an environmental management system that really works. Here are their suggestions.

1. **First consider the areas of largest environmental impact.** Risk Manager Ian McIntosh at Agilent advises, "Draw a circle around your processes and consider all the aspects—as well as the impact of your products during their lifecycle. Consider energy use and hazardous materials." He explains that the South Queensferry, Scotland, facility's environmental management system focuses more on the impact of the site itself

than on its products, in part because only 1,000 units are produced per month (other plants produce millions of units per
month).

2. **Let employees know that the system was created because the organization cares about the environment.** Otherwise, as Danny
   Martland at British Aerospace says, "Cynically, employees can
   say about their company, 'They just want to get certified to
   ISO 14000.'"

3. **Embed the environmental management system's requirements into
   the organization's existing systems.** This practice, seen at nearly
   all the Lean and Green organizations I visited, is more efficient than generating completely different processes.

4. **Have each site or group form a cross-functional team to identify
   gaps between current practices and environmental goals, then have
   the environmental management system fill those gaps.** This rec-
   ommendation, from Texas Instruments, supports the point
   made in Chapter 3: decentralizing environmental control is
   more effective than dictating exactly what each person will do.

5. **Use simple language.** My contacts at NEC say using simple language is effective, especially in countries where environmental protection is not high on the list of social concerns. Michel
   Compérat at Thomson Multimedia gives employees an easy-
   to-read digest of each of ISO 14000's paragraphs. "The ISO
   14000 standards themselves are difficult for the site employees to read," he says.

6. **Check frequently with each of the organization's sites or groups to
   offer help in working with the system.** Michel Compérat not only
   offers help but also arranges for the employees working on

ISO 14000 certification to visit Thomson Multimedia's Poland plant to see the system in action.

7. **Match your employee-training style to your organization's culture.** "In Poland," Compérat says, "the environmental training had to emphasize both at-work and at-home behavior, to convince employees that they have to do something better for the environment."

8. **Get outside help in creating your system.** Ian McKeown of Polaroid received training on quality, safety, and the environment from the Quality College of Scotland.

9. **Roll out the system in phases.** Polaroid's Holland site was the first to be certified to ISO 14000, to be followed by the plant in Scotland. "We're focusing on getting an environmental management system in place for one division of the plant; then we'll roll out the system to the whole plant, and then get the complete site certified," says Ian McKeown.

10. **Add to your first time estimate.** When I first interviewed Linda Gee at LSI Logic, she estimated that because LSI already had set up an environmental management system similar to ISO 14000 "it would take about three months to do our part in certifying to 14000." A few months later Linda changed her estimate to six months: "The registration process takes longer than I originally thought."

Three Pitfalls to Avoid

I have a vested interest in your environmental management system being effective, lest any of your customers, investors, or competitors accuse *you* of all talk and no action and the Lean and Green promise goes unfulfilled at your organization. So I'd like to give you the three best responses to another question I asked during my visits to the Lean and Green organizations: "What mistakes can be made in creating and implementing an environmental management system, and how can these mistakes be avoided?"

1. **Burdening people with bureaucracy** Avoid generating and having to maintain too much documentation in your environmental management system. Keep your plan simple, and include only the procedures and instructions that employees need to implement it. Edan Dionne at IBM recommends that organizations (a) build on existing systems as appropriate, (b) keep it lean, and (c) develop and deploy solutions to common problems as much as possible.

2. **Creating short-lived systems** If you base the system too specifically on current generations of products and services, the system may not apply to your organization a couple of years from now. The system will require a tedious rewrite or grow stale and ineffective. Be broad-minded and forward-thinking in creating yours.

3. **Depending on a single employee** For their environmental management systems, two of the 20 Lean and Green organizations made the mistake of relying solely on an individual employee to create and/or implement it. That person may retire (as happened at Polaroid's Holland site) or move to a different department (as happened at Apple) and leave the rest of the team without the necessary direction or inspiration to continue executing environmental improvements. Remember Lean and Green step 3: Collaborate throughout the organization to meet Lean and Green goals.

Of course mistakes aren't so bad if you learn from them. At both Polaroid and Apple, which long ago abandoned their reliance on a single employee, the environmental management systems are living, breathing, and being implemented throughout the companies. You undoubtedly will make some mistakes in putting together your environmental management system because you and your associates are only human. Just try not to make the three listed above now that you know about them!

Planet-Friendly Plans for Emergencies

Be sure your system includes well-conceived plans to protect the environment in emergency situations. You'll prevent not only environmental harm, but also exorbitant fines, cleanup costs, and possibly harm to human life. At LSI Logic, for example, Linda Gee had me look inside small rooms along the periphery of the plant that were specially constructed to contain a chemical leak, should one occur. "Our first priority is to save human life, second is to protect the environment, and third is to protect our products," she explained. "Fortunately, we have never had to make those priority decisions."

One Company's Environmental Management System Michel Compérat of Thomson Multimedia showed me an inch-thick book of procedures for implementing the company's environ-

> **Prepared for Emergencies?**
>
> Apple's environmental management system analyzes a wide variety of risks by asking tough questions about potential emergencies, no matter how unlikely. "What can the vending-machine delivery person do to impact our site, worst case? Or if 20,000 gallons of diesel oil were spilled, what would happen? What is the maximum foreseeable nightmare?" Bill Brunson says that Apple rates the likelihood and severity of each risk as systematically as possible, then the database rates each risk according to its probability and the severity of the effect. A really unlikely but lethal emergency would be rated low in probability, yet high in severity. Apple considers both environmental and business factors. Brunson says, "Examples of business factors include whether it is a regulatory or legal concern, whether it would affect Apple's image, and its impact on cost."

mental management system. Topics addressed by the system are outlined below. I chose this environmental management system's structure to show you because many of its elements are relevant to a wide range of manufacturing.

1. **Pollution Prevention**
    ▶ Reduce, reuse, and recycle
    ▶ Chemical substitution, reclamation, spill prevention, treatment, and recycling
    ▶ Waste analysis, tracking, and reporting

2. **Hazardous Material Storage**
    ▶ Prevention of spills and accidental releases
    ▶ Proper containment, secondary containment, emergency equipment

3. **Contingency and Emergency Response Plans**
    ▶ Identify and develop written plans for probable emergency situations
    ▶ Preparedness and response plans for hazardous material release, fire, natural disaster, power outage, bomb threat

4. **Hazardous Waste Management**
    ▶ Handling, storage, transportation, and treatment
    ▶ Labels, signs, records, and training

5. **Energy Conservation and Air Management**
    ▶ Management guidelines and conservation measures to maximize energy efficiency
    ▶ Emissions inventory and control technologies

6. **Water Conservation**
    ▶ Identification and implementation of opportunities to minimize consumption

▶ Unauthorized discharge notification

7. **Design for Environment**

   ▶ Integrate environmental considerations into the design process to minimize the environmental impact of the manufacture, use, and eventual disposal of products

8. **Site Acquisition and Closure**

   ▶ Determine extent of environmental assessment or investigation

   ▶ Recordkeeping and closure procedures

MAKING IT EASY

Create a System to Meet Your Environmental Goals

1. Review the sample outline provided on the previous two pages. Which of these elements apply to your organization?

2. Look at your organization's procedures manual, noticing how procedures are organized, explained, and enforced (e.g., does it say three strikes and you're out?). Use a similar style in drafting the first few environmental procedures (e.g., on use of coffee mugs instead of disposable cups) so that other employees can immediately relate to them.

3. Share samples of these drafted procedures with your organization's regional locations, departments, and other groups, asking them to draft procedures for their areas. Reacquaint employees with your organization's Environmental Policy Statement and goals to inspire them to craft forward-thinking, effective policies that foster a Lean and Green organization.

4. Follow up, give positive feedback on what works well in the drafts, and encourage the groups to go slightly Leaner and Greener in areas where you think your organization can do better.

5. Consider getting certified to ISO 14000, especially if this certification is important to your customers, employees, the community, or management.

6. While editing and completing your system, review this chapter's Ten Suggestions for Management Systems and Three Pitfalls to Avoid.

You now have a plan to meet your Lean and Green goals!

Chapter 7

Meet and Exceed Customers' Expectations for Environmental Practices

Our market studies have indicated that environmental performance of our products rated "important" or "very important" in the buying decisions of customers in specific countries.

—Corky Chew, manager of environmental technologies
and strategies, Apple Computer

IT'S likely that some of your best current and prospective customers require you to follow certain environmental practices. You can assure management that if your customers have not yet asked about your organization's green policies, they will. Don't be caught unprepared. Your organization can protect current revenues and grab future sales by being on your customers' lists of suppliers after that list has been environmentally pruned.

Customers Are Speaking Up—Louder Than Regulators

My friend and fellow writer and consultant Byron Swinford asked me recently if I fear that the change from a Democratic to a Republican presidential administration will affect organizations' environmental practices. I was pleased to tell him that I'm not especially concerned—because of the very point made in this chapter: *The world's leading customers now are more environmentally demanding of their suppliers than are government regulations.*

Until the mid-1990s it was unheard of for customers ask their suppliers to complete questionnaires about their environmental practices. Today all of the Lean and Green companies receive such questionnaires. Liz Moyer, corporate environmental, safety, and health policy manager at Texas Instruments, reports that TI annually receives and analyzes approximately 200 environmental surveys and other customer inquiries about the environment. Customers' main interests are the chemicals used in manufacturing, the environmental management system, and the reuse, reduction, and recycling of packaging materials.

Linda Gee at LSI Logic has witnessed this shift from government-regulated to capitalism-induced motivation: "Governmental agencies' environmental regulations are reaching a plateau in terms of requirements; it used to be that every year there was a new regulation. But now, we are getting more requests—indeed perhaps demands—from customers."

I take special delight in this trend. One early impetus to write this book was my learning that the California Circuits Association, whose members are among the most toxic-chemical-intensive firms of the high-tech industry, was spending members' fees to fight the government's environmental regulations. I found this tactic appalling, especially given that earlier reduction of waste and the replacement of environmentally detrimental chemicals by these members would have earned back the association fee by orders of magnitude.

How powerful is the word of the customer for motivating suppliers to be greener? One Lean and Green organization, LSI Logic, actually encourages its customers (including Lean and Green Compaq Computer) to *increase* their environmental requirements of suppliers, to achieve a competitive edge!

Do You Serve the Most Environmentally Demanding Customers—Yet?

If your organization doesn't have customers that care about the environment, don't worry—environmental responsibility isn't important to your marketplace (please hear the sarcasm in this sentence). What *does* the world marketplace think?

► **Europe** "When it comes to customer demand for green products, there is no question that Europe is in the lead on this issue," says Corky Chew at Apple Computer. "We have conducted market surveys in Europe and there is definitely strong support for inclusion of environmental attributes into our products. This customer demand is so strong that, everything else being equal, customers are willing to pay more for an 'eco-labeled' computer." Eco-labels signify that a product meets the environmental attributes specific to that label; they are issued by governments, companies, and associations of organizations.

► **Asia** Polaroid's Ian McKeown says, "Companies in Japan are trying to get into Fortress Europe by getting their plants certified to environmental standard ISO 14000 and getting the CE mark [an eco-label that also covers electrical interference and safety; see Glossary] for their products." According to Tom Zeilinski at ITT Gilfillan, customers in Taiwan are especially interested in environmental improvements because Taiwan is an island, with particular vulnerability to air and water pollution.

► **North America** In the United States, the Environmental Protection Agency's Energy Star requires the lowest-to-date energy consumption for products (two to three watts for standby power). This limit may soon be reduced (to one watt) by European and Japanese television makers. In the United States, most would attest that California is among the most demanding, surpassed only by New Jersey, which has stricter standards for water purity. Canadian customers' environmental requirements are at least equal to those in the United States.

▶ **Latin America** With Mexico City in crisis over deaths caused by egregious air pollution, Mexico is fighting to employ the same environmental practices that more developed countries use. The president of Costa Rica, Dr. Miguel Angel Rodriguez, told me in 1999 that "industry and the environment are not incompatible. In fact, it can be good for business to be environmentally protective." One of his top seven goals for his country is environmental sustainability: 25 percent of the world's tropical biological research is conducted in Costa Rica.

▶ **New Zealand** What seems radical to most of us environmentally was already in place in New Zealand by 1990.

▶ **Banks, telecommunications companies, schools, and retail** These are the toughest industries, according to Compaq's analysis of its customers' environmental questionnaires.

▶ **The oil and gas industry** Exxon's environmental questionnaire is rigorous, and it's no wonder, given that Exxon has been responsible for creating a Superfund site and wants to ensure that its suppliers follow strict environmental guidelines. (The EPA's Superfund program locates, investigates, and oversees the cleanup of sites where uncontrolled or abandoned hazardous wastes threaten the public health or environment; also see Glossary.)

▶ **The high-tech industry** You may have noticed by now that many of the Lean and Green companies discussed in this book are in the high-tech industry. It's no accident. The high-tech industry tends to lead change. So as the high-tech industry does, so will most of *your* customers in a few years.

I'm sure you get the point. The myth that environmental moves are bad for business can be forever dispelled given that customers around the world and in nearly every region are creating a competitive edge for suppliers who are meeting higher environmental standards.

Beware of customers passing the buck! If you're not savvy to it, some customers could try to push *their* environmental issues onto *your* organization. Chuck Taylor, manager of environmental, health, and safety at ITT Cannon, told me, "One customer wanted us to build a connector because they didn't want to have to deal with the hazardous materials at their own site." Work with the customer to find an arrangement in which both your companies—and the environment—can win.

Training *Customers* in Green Practices

To meet your organization's Lean and Green goals, you may find yourself training customers to take environmental steps. One year, Frank O'Rourke at Celestica's Canadian headquarters had a goal of reducing his facility's $2 million chemical budget by $125,000. "We try to convince customers to switch from brand X to brand Y if we know that Y will be better environmentally and economically," says O'Rourke. "We show the customer our test results with Y and report that it's less expensive." For example, some customers want Celestica to use water-soluble paste or flux, instead of chemicals, as the basis for a water-cleaning process.

Celestica then encourages customers to go even further to reduce cost and use of resources by switching to a "no-clean" process.

You can make a more positive impact on the environment than you realize when you inform customers about the environmentally beneficial options. When Celestica convinces a customer to make environmental improvements, the positive impact is even greater than usual, because Celestica helps to design, manufacture, and ship its customers' own name-brand products all over the world. I asked Frank O'Rourke if he predicts that his environmental suggestions to customers will continue to meet with acceptance. "I think I'll make my chemical-reduction goal," he says.

Using Eco-Labels to Tell Customers about Green Products

One easy way to inform customers that your product meets their environmental requirements is to affix an eco-label to it. Eco-labels, usually issued by a government agency or an industry group, certify that a product performs with minimal negative impact on the environment. For example, I am writing this book with the assistance of a Toshiba Libretto 110 CT laptop computer, which has an Energy Star sticker on it from the U.S. Environmental Protection Agency.

The idea of eco-labels sounds good so far, right? But the disadvantages of eco-labels are many—starting with there being too many of them. Even though for two years in a row the EPA named Compaq the Energy Star PC Partner of the Year, some of Compaq's European customers also wanted the Swedish TCO '95 eco-label on Compaq's monitors.

Some individual countries' eco-labels are tough to get administratively. A client of mine in Silicon Valley called me with urgency and frustration in her voice: "I want to get the Blue

Angel eco-label for my products, but I can't seem to get a copy of the instructions and application. I received an old one, but it's out of date. And the current one is only in German!" We got the new regulations for her—in English. Candidates for Germany's Blue Angel eco-label need to complete an application and go through an approval process, including getting statements from suppliers. Initially the specifications were released only in German, but the organizers soon realized that to encourage non-German companies to qualify it was not in their best interest to keep the specifications in German only.

Another issue with eco-labels was brought out by Michel Compérat at Thomson Multimedia. He says a label such as the Energy Star is meant to reward the energy efficiency of one product, rather than a range of products—and even less the whole production philosophy of a manufacturer. "The label is fine in itself," he observes, "but does not entail that the manufacturer is committed to reduce energy consumption. It just means that one particular product has been designed to suit the tastes of energy-consumption-conscious consumers—a marketing niche, no more, no less."

Compérat says that a voluntary agreement issued by the European Association of Consumer Electronic Manufacturers, signed by Thomson Multimedia and nearly two dozen other companies, helps to ensure that environmental improvements are made across companies' entire product lines. "From an industrial perspective," he says, "the voluntary agreement reflects a commitment to globally achieve results and preserve energy, inducing a 'pull' effect, which is a very different approach from eco-labeling, where ultimately the individual consumer is left to decide among products, inducing a 'push' effect of uncertain magnitude." After signing the voluntary agreement, Thomson

Multimedia reduced the average power consumption of its TVs and VCRs by 30 percent over a two-year period.

To further complicate the issue in consumers' minds, some individual companies put eco-labels on their own products. At Kyocera, for example, products that meet the company's internally set standards can use the Kyocera Eco-Product mark.

Yes, eco-labels have the disadvantage of being awarded for meeting different environmental requirements in different countries; and sometimes the approval processes are arduous. But in my mind the positives outweigh the negatives: as customers accelerate their preferences for products sporting eco-labels, it becomes all the more obvious to see the competitive advantage that Lean and Green companies own.

MAKING IT EASY

**Please Customers, Benefit the Environment,
and Increase Profits**

1. Start by reviewing your customers' or constituents' environmental concerns, which they have expressed through questionnaires, letters, or other means.

2. Make a list of customers your organization would like to have, and ask them what they care about environmentally as it pertains to organizations they patronize. Yes, go ahead and ask them — they'll be pleased that you are proactive.

3. Prioritize the list of customers' environmental concerns and interests, and make these your organization's priorities too.

4. Consider LSI Logic's strategy: ensure that your Lean and Green practices are ahead of your competition's, and encourage your customers to increase their environmental requirements of suppliers.

You now have a competitive edge!

Chapter 8
Translate Green Practices into Revenues

If you consider the total cost of one TV set from production, through ownership, to the end of ownership, only 15 percent of the cost is associated with manufacturing; 85 percent comes from electricity and other running costs. So from a global perspective, when Sony designs and manufactures TV sets that consume less electricity during ownership, Sony is contributing more to overall energy savings.

— Nobuyuki Watanabe, vice president,
Corporate Environmental Affairs, Sony

CUSTOMERS like to save money; there is little doubt about that. Whereas *some* people are willing to pay more for green products—for example, a majority of Americans say they would spend more to buy energy-efficient kitchen appliances or a vehicle with higher fuel economy (according to Oxygen TV's web site, www.oxygen.com, January 2001)—some are *not* willing to pay more. The good news is that *green products often do save customers money* because they use fewer materials in the product, generate less waste during manufacturing, and cost less to operate. Now that's a point that sets on shaky ground the myth that businesses can be only Lean *or* Green.

This chapter shows you that Lean and Green step 1—questioning wasteful practices and designing products to benefit profit and planet—can create "green revenue." Selling green products, recycling, and other revenue-earning strategies can be just as key to your organization's profitability as reducing costs. Also, see how the marketers of Lean and Green products featured in this chapter encourage customers to buy green products based on the cost savings they'll enjoy (step 2—using business language to encourage green decisions).

Selling Green Products

If you have any doubt that green products are giving some organizations a competitive edge, consider these true stories:

► Horizon Organic Dairy is the largest company in an industry (organic dairies) that attracts customers primarily for environmental and health reasons. In 1999 Horizon Organic Dairy experienced annual sales growth of 70 percent—in the same year that total milk production shrank by 3 percent (according to the National Agricultural Statistics Services, a division of the U.S. Department of Agriculture), even though prices for organic dairy products often are *higher* than for their conventional counterparts.

► Kyocera's ECOSYS page printer, the first to receive Germany's Blue Angel eco-label, garners a 12 percent market share in Germany, where corporations are conscious about protecting the environment, and 7 percent Europe-wide. The printer uses original technology, including long-life amorphous silicon drums, to eliminate the need for replacement parts. And when the printer needs more toner (ink), instead of replacing an entire cartridge, only the toner container is replaced. According to Kyocera, these environmental features make per-page printing cost one-eighth the cost of printing a page using a competing printer (based on printing 2,000 pages per month).

► A group boycotting a particular retail chain for buying and selling old-growth lumber posted an Internet notice praising Louisiana-Pacific lumber products for being environmentally sound. According to Liz Smith, LP's director of environmental affairs, their boards often are made from logs as small as four inches in diameter, or from waste or recycled wood fiber. Not many processes can use these small trees, which are removed to thin a young forest and give remaining trees room to grow. This process makes for healthy forests and affordable building products.

► Philips Semiconductor's GreenChip™ increases the energy efficiency of televisions. The company is so convinced of the competitive edge this product gives Philips in the marketplace that Philips is protecting the product's intellectual property with patents; it has received 12 so far. More about *how* Philips's GreenChip™ improves the environmental performance of consumer products is in Chapter 9.

► Henk de Bruin at Philips's corporate office says, "Green products have lower bills of materials [fewer items to purchase thus less expense] and in some places increased market share and a price premium. So the business benefit of producing green products is a no-brainer because you always win on materials." De Bruin says that the fluorescent bulb use in Philips's Alto lamp is a good example: "You can't eliminate mercury [a hazardous substance] completely, but we reduced the mercury in the bulb by 80 percent, which reduces Philips's costs significantly. For a distinguishing marketing feature, we paint the caps green. This product has been a big success in the U.S. market. Our competitors can't keep up."

▶ Danny Martland at British Aerospace says, "Our civil aircraft is very, very fuel efficient." British Aerospace has a 40 percent share in the partnership with France and Germany to produce the Airbus civil aircraft. "Airbus products are outselling Boeing now because customers want the cost advantages of fuel efficiency," says Martland. "Some civil airlines are starting to ask environmental questions, such as 'What are you doing about use of cadmium?' and asking if in the final assembly of civil aircraft we're using environmentally friendly paints and fewer solvents."

Sometimes green products do cost more than conventional ones. But some of the green products listed above are successful *despite* their higher prices to consumers. The selling point generally is a clear promise of lower costs over the life of the product. Kyocera's ECOSYS printer, for example, is priced 20 percent higher than the competition's products, mainly because the printer is designed to be disassembled by type of material for easier recycling at the end of the product's life; this green feature adds to manufacturing costs. Soon, however, other companies will need to follow suit in light of the end-of-product-life regulation (described in Chapter 12). Notwithstanding the higher price tag, ECOSYS has succeeded in the marketplace, according to our contacts at Kyocera, owing to its lower operating costs—again based on environmental design improvements.

What products and services does your organization offer, or do you consume, that can boast use of fewer manufacturing or usage resources? Perhaps your organization already markets a green product and you've just not featured it as such. By publicizing its green qualities you could increase your market share. Or better yet, perhaps this book is giving you ideas for making your products and services Leaner and Greener. This way, you could make a significant improvement to the health of the environment and your organization's financial returns.

Revenue from Recycling

A less dramatic source of revenue compared to selling green products is earning money through recycling materials. Recycling can fund parties, of course, but it can also cause materials to be reused that otherwise would end up in burgeoning landfills or being incinerated and contributing to air pollution.

Frank O'Rourke of Celestica started to receive checks from his group's recycling efforts, but being in operations he had no idea where (into what account) to deposit these checks. So Celestica's finance and accounts payable department set up an internal account code for recycling revenue. The checks deposited into that account, from recycling manufacturing and office materials, now total about a half-million dollars a year.

One of Celestica's more lucrative recycling efforts—which generates revenue of $200,000 a year in Canadian dollars (about U.S.$135,000)—is selling dross from wave solder machines and solder paste that according to Celestica's standards is expired (because it's been out of the refrigerator more than four hours) but that to companies with less stringent specifications is usable. "One of my goals," says Frank O'Rourke, "was to increase solder-paste recycling revenue. I went to three or four suppliers saying I wanted a better price for a single deal in which they would sell paste to Celestica and also buy back expired/recycled material. So now we get a better price on new materials and more revenue for recycling."

Nirmal Singh at ITT Cannon explains that his company earns revenue from recycling of dozens of types of materials: "We get money back from selling aluminum chips left over from our

A Green Television

A Thomson Multimedia promotional brochure uses arrows to point to all of the environmentally friendly features of one of its televisions:

▶ At least 20 percent of the plastic used is recycled.
▶ All plastics used are compatible with recycling.
▶ No bromide is used in the plastics.
▶ Labels are made of compatible plastics.
▶ The chassis frame is made of 100 percent recycled plastic.
▶ There is no cadmium in the tube.
▶ There is no paint on the product.
▶ The packaging is 100 percent recyclable.
▶ The polystyrene used in the packaging is 100 percent recycled.

The promotional piece also proudly proclaims: "A TV at the forefront of environmental protection," and "We must achieve the target of producing more while consuming fewer natural resources and ensuring our products are responsibly designed to minimize the environmental impact until recycling at end of life."

machining operations." He adds, though, that it's more important to focus on saving costs than on earning revenues through environmental measures.

Other Revenue Benefits of Going Green

If your organization does not yet have green products or services to sell, and if recycling revenue is minor or nonexistent, consider developing some less tangible but nonetheless important sources of revenue by paying attention to customers' green desires.

▶ **Public image** Walt Rosenberg at Compaq believes that people underestimate how much the environment influences a buyer's decision: "Customers have an emotional reaction when there's an environmental mistake." He adds, "Some liberal magazines give us insight on what issues are starting to be elevated. Representatives from the Sierra Club came inside for a few days to look at Compaq's programs and processes—Sierra Club became a new friend. This is one reason we put our environmental action on our website."

▶ **Avoiding loss of potential revenue owing to production delays** Dawne Schomer, director of Texas Instruments' corporate environmental, safety, and health program, gave this response when I asked whether the company has generated revenue through green activities: "Every day that a permit for a new facility is delayed because a member of the community holds it up—based on reading an article about the environmental harms of manufacturing—can be expensive for TI." This "delayed revenue" proposition, among other reasons, has encouraged the company to choose chemicals and gases that "get us off the regulators' radar screens" and make environmental choices "that barrel us ahead of community concerns."

▶ **Making money from selling your Lean and Green processes** A couple of Kyocera's green products came from the company's own emphasis on energy-efficient internal operations, for which it developed co-generation and solar-energy hybrid systems for its own use. Since then, Kyocera has been selling these products commercially, generating enough revenues for Kyocera to recoup its development costs.

MAKING IT EASY

Enhance Revenues while Enhancing the Planet

1. Spend two or three hours calling all the recyclers in your community to make a list of everything they buy. In my community, the phone book has a listing for "Recycling." Compare that list with your company's waste and start earning money.

2. Consider what your customers or constituents value most. If "smaller size," "lighter weight," or "less expensive to run" is among their desires, you have an opportunity to provide them with a greener solution. Your costs may even be less.

3. If your selling cost for the green product or service is higher than your competitors', start by charging more and emphasize the customer benefits (better size, less expensive to operate, etc.).

4. Be sure that any claims you make about your product or service's environmental benefits are true. If they are not, the negative publicity stemming from the discovery of your false statements will hurt your business.

5. Keep excellent records of the money you are earning through recycling and the revenue and profitability of the green products and services. Use these records to inspire top management to become even Leaner and Greener.

Now you are earning revenue from your environmental steps.

Chapter 9

Design Resource Savings into Products and Processes

> Pushing technology is one of the main ways to achieve profitable
> environmental steps—to become a leading-edge user. Even
> though Kyocera may have to pay a higher price for designing
> such technology, investing early gives Kyocera an early return.
>
> — Hisashi Sakumi, general manager,
> General Affairs Division, Kyocera

THE Lean and Green ideas that most benefit the environment and your organization's profitability are those implemented at the early stage of product or process design. "Designing for the environment" means thinking environmentally early in a product's lifetime—at the time of design. It is at this early stage that environmental problems or waste can be avoided *before* they occur. Thomson Multimedia's Michel Compérat says, "I prefer to work at the origin of the pollution."

The benefits of solving environmental issues at the design phase, according to Diana Lyon at IBM, number at least three:

1. Staying ahead of regulations. For example, IBM designed—before it was required—a secondary containment system to catch any spilled chemicals during the delivery of chemicals to some of its manufacturing plants.

2. Improving profit margins by reducing expenses. Fines for chemical spills and the cost of cleanup afterward would have counted directly toward expenses and against profit. The secondary containment system precluded those expenses.

3. Reducing consumption of water, packaging, and chemicals.

Read on to see numerous examples of early design changes that reduced forever the need for precious natural resources, unnecessary purchases, and hazardous materials.

An example from IBM of the third benefit comes from its printed-circuit-board plant in Yasu, Japan. By designing a dry-polishing technique that replaced a wet-scrubbing process, IBM saved $2.2 million in water in only two years and eliminated the need to build an $18 million water supply and treatment facility.

For this chapter, I've chosen my favorite design changes that the 20 Lean and Green organizations have made. What unites most of them is use of new technology plus a willingness to question deeply the wasteful practices of the past—Lean and Green step 1.

Designing *Process* for Environmental Benefit and Lower Costs

No matter what your organization does or how large or small it is, your organization has processes—either by default or according to formal instructions—for taking almost every action, from assembling items sold to customers, to paying bills, to communicating with people inside and outside the organization. I promise you that by stepping back and looking objectively at the processes your organization employs you will find some wasted resources and opportunities to achieve Lean and Green results.

Ian McKeown at Polaroid in Scotland observed a process at his company, then made it Leaner and Greener to the tune of reducing costs by 20 percent, shortening manufacturing time, and improving the environment. He explains, "We used to have assembly lines in which employees passed along cameras in various stages of assembly from one station to another—even if the parts were defective, and the products had to be thrown away at the end of the assembly line." You can imagine how wasteful this was. By questioning this practice, McKeown found a better way: "Then, we started using better materials and created groups of only two or three people who each assemble considerable portions of the cameras while standing and moving through their work areas. The assemblers do their own testing during the assembly process, so they do not have to wait for others to perform tests; this used to be a bottleneck. They pass along only good materials to the next person. This process continually reduces waste, time, and inventory. We've reduced the cost of manufacturing by 20 percent."

ITT Gilfillan in California provides another example of Lean and Green process redesign. Bob Barrett at ITT Gilfillan was tasked with reducing chemical use: "From developing an inventory of what we used and where, I found out we used chemicals everywhere! We created in the early 1990s what became known as the 'List of 23'—chemicals targeted for elimination or reduction. We ranked them by amount of use, level of toxicity, and ease of replacement, then wrote a master plan for eliminating each of them." Bob says that many of the 23 chemicals were replaced with relatively inexpensive commercial detergents, for which disposal costs are minimal and initial equipment costs were a wash (a pun from Bob's boss, Tom Zeilinski). In addition, Bob eliminated costly and time-consuming chemical permits. The green results of replacing toxic chemicals are obvious. What were the lean results? Gilfillan avoided $370,000 in purchases and toxic chemical disposal costs over five years. For example, one 55-gallon drum of compound 1,1,1 trichloroethane (one of the 23 replaced chemicals) cost $6,400 to purchase and another $5,000 in excise taxes.

Use Design-for-Environment Foresight Is your industry one that plans new generations of products and services well into the future? If so, the Lean and Green ideas you think of today can propel organizational and environmental health well into the next decade. For example, at Intel environmental and other design factors are considered in tandem with processing, purchasing, and other functions—years ahead of product release. Jim Larsen says, "We're working now on products and processes to prepare for global climate change regulations with deadlines of 8 to 12 years from now." Designing green manufacturing processes for so many product generations ahead also saves money earlier on: Intel was able to eliminate PFCs (perfluorocarbons, global-warming chemicals) five product generations ahead, and in the meantime avoided buying expensive equipment to abate the emissions.

Skip Over Unnecessary Processes My friends and colleagues call me an "efficiency queen," and I have to admit that I enjoy discovering ways to eliminate unnecessary steps to arrive more quickly and easily at the desired result. Now that you know this about me, you'll understand why I particularly like this story from ITT Gilfillan. When Bob Barrett started at Gilfillan, the company regularly used chemicals because they were efficient—as many as seven chemical cleanings were used in some operations. Bob says, "No one questioned it." When he became more aware of protecting the environment, Bob asked himself, "Why do we have to clean seven times?" He says, "The way to design change is not to think in stages but instead think first about the end. Instead of replacing one solvent with a less-toxic solvent, which eventually will be banned, go all the way to soap and water or no cleaning at all." Going from seven chemical cleaning stages to none. Now that's efficient.

Designing the *Product* to be Leaner and Greener

Now let's shift our focus from designing *processes* with the environment and cost savings in mind to designing Lean and Green *products*. Philips in Holland provides my favorite example. I predict that you will be impressed, as I was, by the far-reaching benefits to our planet—and also to customers—of a two-ounce semiconductor chip.

Ton Mobers at Philips's Nijmegen, Holland, site, told me, "In our business, environmental focus gets into our product mainly because of cost-reduction efforts. The environment receives benefit—but not for idealism. It's for cost and efficiency." For the GreenChip™ family of semiconductors, Mobers and his design team did something extra for marketing purposes: they made improvements to the standby power mode. "Standby" is when a videocassette recorder, television, or computer monitor is plugged in but not turned on—which on average is at least 50 percent of the time. I was fascinated as Mobers and his colleagues sat around the table listing benefit after benefit for the environment as well as Philips's and its customers' profitability, as I've summarized below.

▶ **Uses less power** When a TV contains a Philips GreenChip™, the TV needs only 1.5 to 2 watts of electricity, which is ten times less than a standard product in the standby mode. This saves customers significant energy cost and conserves nonrenewable energy sources.

▶ **Increases speed for customers; reduces consumption of materials** The GreenChip™ was designed to be 2,000 times faster than older TV chips. This speed is not only good for customers, but also it allows a large TV component—the transformer—to be smaller and less expensive.

▶ **Produces less power** Mobers and his team have a new chip that cuts in half the heat generated by a TV. This increases the product's life span and requires fewer components (such as heat sinks) to dissipate all that heat. The TV can be smaller, lighter, and cost less to consumers.

▶ **Increases product reliability** Because Philips's new semiconductor chips are "smarter" than previous chips, 40 fewer components are needed to run the TV than competitors need in their current models. Think of the advantages of having fewer parts: simpler-to-design products; less to purchase, stock, and track; and less to fail.

▶ **Decreases manufacturing costs** Because TVs containing Philips's GreenChip™ use less power, generate less heat, and use fewer parts, the TV maker saves money and time in assembling them.

▶ **Increases safety** By reducing the number of components needed, increasing speed, and reducing both power consumption and generation, the product becomes more robust and reliable, which translates into safety. Philip's GreenChip™ is short-circuit-proof, according to Mobers, is protected from over- or under-voltage and from over-current, and has a temperature cut-off. A German TV maker designed in the GreenChip™ primarily for this safety feature.

▶ **Reduces transportation costs** The smaller, lighter TV has additional environmental and business benefits. Fifteen TVs fit on one shipping tray instead of only 10, as discovered by a TV maker in Taiwan. A small truck instead of a big truck can transport the same number of TVs.

Even though Ton Mobers at Philips downplayed environmental benefits as the main reason for designing most chips, he grew passionate when he described what this power savings means in the aggregate: "You can look at it this way: Switching to energy-efficient products would allow the United States to close four nuclear power plants." That's in a developed nation. He also noted the impact that energy conservation could have in a developing nation: "If people in China choose energy-efficient products for their first TV sets, it would mean not having to build as many power plants there to begin with."

Training Designers to Think Lean and Green

After reading about the Philips Lean and Green chip, *you* might be convinced that designing environment into processes and products makes an enormous impact on profit and planet. But how can you get your colleagues to share your enthusiasm for Lean and Green design?

Encouraging people to make just about any kind of change starts with sharing a vision, providing training and support, and setting expectations. Bob Helms, VP of worldwide research and development at Texas Instruments, shared with me a vision for change that I wish would be adopted by *all* organizations around the globe. Bob says, "Imagine a TI engineer walking into work on any given day and starting to develop new processes or technology. I want him or her to balance environmental factors equally with all other factors considered. We need that balance to generate the right solutions for TI, and at the end of the line they will be the most cost-effective solutions as well."

MAKING IT EASY

Design Waste Out and Profitability In

1. Walk through a couple of your organization's processes (you may need to ask others to describe how things are currently done). With the benefit of a fresh perspective, ask yourself, "To accomplish what's needed, how would I reduce waste, increase efficiency, and ultimately save money?"

2. Now, consider the materials purchased by your organization. Ask your designers about replacing or eliminating materials or parts whose use leaves the greatest environmental footprint.

3. Turn your attention now to the *use* of your organization's products and services — their impact on the environment when in use and after use. Ask your designers what they can do to minimize this impact. Chances are the changes will reduce costs for your company or your customers, or both!

4. If your company custom-manufactures products for other organizations, convince your customer that the earlier he or she delivers the initial design requirements to you, the sooner you can "design for the environment" and realize cost savings for the customer.

5. If you work for a service organization, think about the "design" of the components of the service. At my consulting firm, we used to deliver our studies and recommendations in plastic spiral-bound notebooks; now we use e-mail nearly exclusively, saving time, money, paper, and nonrecyclable plastic.

You now are using green designs to reduce waste and save time, money, and precious natural resources.

Chapter 10
Reduce: The Best Strategy in the RRR Trilogy

Conventional rhetoric, propagated by the chemical industry, is
that if all farms went organic, the world would starve because of
lower yields. We've proved that we are just as productive without
using antibiotics, hormones, or pesticides.

  —Barney Little, general manager, Horizon Organic Dairy

I CALL "reducing, reusing, and recycling materials" the RRR trilogy for Lean and Green results. Chapters 10, 11, and 12 describe how this trilogy spawns dramatic profit *and* environmental benefits through Lean and Green step 1: Question wasteful practices, and design Lean and Green steps to benefit profit and planet. Why reduce, reuse, and recycle? Because these activities diminish organizations' impact on the planet *and* save or earn money.

▶ **Reduce** If you don't have to buy it, don't. Your organization will not only purchase fewer resources, but also not have to deal with those resources after use.

▶ **Reuse** If you have to buy it, use it well and find other uses for the same materials. You'll consume fewer resources and delay or avoid sending them to the landfill or incinerator.

▶ **Recycle** If you have to buy it and cannot reuse it yourself, then convert the material into something else. You'll earn revenues and keep the item out of a landfill or incinerator temporarily or permanently.

Why "Reduce" Is the First Choice for Profit and Planet

Of the RRR Trilogy—reduce, reuse, and recycle—reduce should be your first choice for profit and planet, because even better than purchasing an item and reusing or recycling it is not having to purchase it in the first place. "At Philips, we say less is better," says Henk de Bruin. "Less is better means that we can achieve more functions and intelligence in our electronic products with less material. Less is better also means that you can deliver a higher-value-added product."

Reduce Water In California, we joke about having four seasons: earthquake, fire, mudslide, and drought. As California's population continues to grow, drought has the longest lasting implications of these four. In New Mexico and Israel—where some of Intel's plants are located—water scarcity is particularly keen. You can help by seeing where your organization uses water and—as a young process engineer at Texas Instruments did—find ways to minimize water use.

Claire Jung at Texas Instruments has figured out how to decrease cost per semiconductor wafer (a thin disk from which semiconductor chips are sliced) and process more wafers with the same equipment (increasing productivity) by using 65 fewer gallons per minute of fresh city water. The savings is near $100,000 per quarter in the cost of purchasing water, not including the savings from eliminating treatment and discharge of the water. When process improvements reduced 25 gallons per minute,

Jung's boss bought everyone pizza. Employees asked, "What if we hit 75 gallons?" He said, "That's too easy. If you hit 100 gallons per minute we'll go out for steak and ale."

My job in researching this book was to be a skeptic, so I asked how much money Claire Jung and the team spent to develop and maintain these water-saving processes. They told me that testing the process each year costs $60,000 to $100,000, so payback takes less than four months. When this plant's methods are fanned out to other TI facilities, the payback will be even greater. Also, I saw how using less water for rinsing parts eliminates manufacturing bottlenecks—getting finished products to the market faster, for faster collection of revenues.

Reduce Gas and Electricity Because TI tracks cost savings so precisely, let's stay with Texas Instruments for an example of reducing energy use. TI measures utility cost per semiconductor wafer—including gas and electricity used not only in the manufacturing process itself but also in cafeterias and marketing centers—because these are seen as costs of doing business. A utility steering team was formed to contribute to TI's Zero Zero goal of producing "zero waste." TI reduced energy use by 45 percent during that effort, then later reduced energy use by another 22 percent. How would *you* like to shave this much off *your* organization's energy bill?

Reduce Plastic Packaging I found this next resource-reduction success in France. Thomson Multimedia reduced the mass of one piece of plastic packaging used to protect televisions during shipping by 43 percent. How? Someone thought of replacing the solid piece of packaging with a hollow frame that protects the television just as well. Here's an even more significant reduction of plastic materials at the same company: a rectangular piece of plastic packaging comprising 700 grams of virgin materials was redesigned in the shape of an hourglass comprising 330 grams of 100 percent recycled materials. Not only was the plastic mass reduced by 52 percent, but the new design also made good use of recycled materials.

To ship fragile high-end disk drives, IBM replaced nonrecyclable polyurethane die-cut foam cushioning with 100 percent post-consumer polyethylene that is recycled from milk jugs and beverage bottles. Diana Lyon says, "The new package is reusable and recyclable, and the waste it avoids would fill a football field 4.8 feet deep every year." Plus, the new packaging costs less than the foam it replaced, and its design and increased density also save storage and transportation costs. The new packaging saves IBM $2.7 million annually.

Reduce Paper Chances are you already are reducing your paper purchases by using the back side of scratch paper and using e-mail more than snail mail. Here is an idea—from Lean and Green organization Polaroid—that can significantly reduce the use of paper for all of us who take photographs. According to Ian McKeown, "The trend is for more focus on imaging and electronics transferring of information, so fewer hard copies are produced, meaning that less paper is used. The more computers are used—especially on the desktop—the less printing of photographs is required. Instead of taking three rolls of printed photos, take one photo and before printing it modify it to look just right on the screen." You may be able to change your organization's processes or products—as in Ian's example—to reduce the need for paper on a planetary scale.

Reduce Chemicals Here is some environmentally and profit-minded advice: *Get rid of your hazardous chemicals as quickly as you possibly can!* Hazardous chemicals are called that because they are hazardous to the health of humans, animals, plants, soil, water, air, and ozone. They also are expensive to purchase, transport, store, get permits for, use, and dispose of.

Chances are that you don't need too much convincing that hazardous chemicals are antithetical to being Lean and Green. "But how can you just get rid of them," you ask, "when they are used for so many applications and for decades have been propagated by large, powerful chemical companies?" Replacing these chemicals is easier than you'd think. Consider these examples from two Lean and Green organizations.

An innovation in IBM's printer manufacturing process in Endicott, New York, is a good case study for seeing just how much environmental impact and money is saved by eliminating a chemical. By using oxygen to regenerate ferric chloride, which etches letter characters into stainless steel print bands, IBM saved $600,000 by avoiding buying 750,000 gallons of the virgin etchant, and saved another $1.5 million by eliminating 7,500 tons of waste treatment sludge. When the Endicott plant bought and installed the regeneration system for $250,000, a 150 percent return on investment was expected; in practice IBM has so far received an 840 percent return!

TI's VP of Worldwide Facilities, Shaunna Sowell, eloquently describes numerous examples of the Lean and Green promise; the ease with which old processes can be replaced with cleaner ones surprised even her: "We showed our designers a list of 50 chemicals—from 10,000 chemicals that TI uses for everything from washroom soap to glue in desk drawers—we wanted to remove from our process. The 50 comprised known carcinogens or otherwise needed to be reported in compliance with the Clean Air Act. We thought it would take 6 to 12 months to design out as many of the 50 chemicals that were possible to avoid. The design team came back to us in two months saying, 'We found substitutions for 49 of the chemicals, but it'll take a year for the 50th.' We were stunned and asked, 'How did you do it?' They replied, 'Look, this early in the design we've got lots of choices; we know what is good for processes, but we didn't know what worked for the environment and health. We care too, but just didn't know which chemicals were on the list.'" Shaunna had wondered, "Where have we been? We could have done this earlier. In two months of work that cost TI next to nothing, we designed out significant costs for the next ten years."

Reduce Lead One of the most challenging materials to reduce and eventually try to eliminate is lead, which poisons water and soil to the detriment of sea life and humans alike. The U.S. Centers for Disease Control and Prevention considers lead poisoning to be the number-one preventable health problem facing children. Low-dose exposure to lead—from lead-based paint, ambient air, indoor dust, and soil—can cause decreased attention span, hyperactivity, and low IQ scores (see the article "Relationship between Lead Mining and Blood Level in Children" by Ana Maria Murgueytio in *Environmental Health*, November 1998). One would hope that the environmental and health arguments for the use of lead in manufacturing would be enough to prompt management to make immediate changes. But I personally have seen a remarkable amount of resistance even among electronics executives I admire. Thank goodness for the "End of Life Electrical and Electronic Equipment"

European directive, formulated by the European Community, which is forcing the issue by banning the use of lead in new equipment. See how the Lean and Green champions are getting the lead out in their operations.

Perhaps most challenging is the global move to remove the lead from the tin-lead solder that connects components inside electronic products (its makeup is 37 percent lead). Alternative metals' higher melting temperatures wreak havoc with components not able to withstand the heat that makes solder molten. Linda Klober, manager of process engineering and development at Celestica, looked at conductive adhesives with researchers at the University of Toronto, but none could survive thermal cycling. In the meantime, while Celestica is looking at leadless solder, Celestica is recycling lead-tin solder paste and dross (solder with contaminant). I have great hopes that Klober and her team will find a lead-free solution, given that in 1991 she spearheaded a creative effort to eliminate CFC (ozone-depleting) cleaning chemicals with a process that requires no cleaning at all. Think how this solution will create Lean (chemical reduction) and Green (no equipment, chemicals, or processing to pay for) benefits!

Lead is also used in bar stock for machining aluminum parts in a wide range of industries. Nirmal Singh at ITT Cannon explains, "The aluminum bar has lead in it so it's not so brittle. Die-cast aluminum is lead-free. We're reviewing how much lead we use, customer by customer. Cadmium plating will withstand saltwater for four days; we can sell the same connector with an anodized plating or plastics if the connectors are not used in harsh environments." For one of Cannon's product lines, silver solder is used instead of lead solder. Rosin is still required, but it is cleaned with Citri-Clean, a biodegradable cleaning solution comprising citrus oil instead of toxic solvents.

Reduce Consumption of Fossil Fuels and Air Pollution Most of us expect our heaters and cars to start up whenever we need them. But the fact is that fossil fuels—oil and gas—will be depleted on the planet within 300 years. The Los Angeles basin will run out of oil in less than 50 years. And if this timeline is too long to motivate some people to take action today, then consider that in some regions the burning of fossil fuels is already responsible for air so polluted that children and elderly people have gotten sick and died. And if financial arguments speak loudest to you, consider the rising costs and intermittent supply of oil, along with the political turbulence it generates. All of these are good reasons for organizations to reduce their reliance on fossil fuels for health, planet, operational risk management, and cost reductions.

Several of the Lean and Green organizations, including Sony, ITT Cannon, and the city of Santa Monica, have reduced their use of fossil fuels by switching to electric and other alternative vehicles. For maintenance outside the plant, ITT Cannon uses electric carts instead of gas-powered vehicles. Soon the carts will be powered by solar panels, to take advantage of the sunny southern California climate. Nirmal Singh smiled when he said, "I like to rub this in when I talk with sister divisions on the East Coast." Dean Kubani gave me a tour of Santa Monica in one of the city's many electric vehicles: 65 percent of Santa Monica's city fleet is electric or runs on fuels other than gas and diesel. Because more and more of the city's vehicles run on natural gas, this city built its own tank and pump system.

Get Employees Out of Their Cars!

The solo commuter is a significant contributor to traffic congestion and smoggy skies: automobiles contribute 40 percent of the reactive hydrocarbons, 73 percent of the nitrogen oxides, and 90 percent of the carbon monoxide polluting the air today (LSI Logic's website—www.LSIL.com, 1999). So, before concluding this chapter on reducing resource consumption—the most important strategy in the RRR Trilogy—let me suggest some ways you can encourage employees to minimize use of nonrenewable resources and reduce pollution when commuting to work:

► Provide a ride-matching service for employees who want to carpool, and e-mail employees before a "Spare the Air" day (days on which local agencies predict high air pollution levels) to encourage employees to carpool especially on those days. (LSI Logic does this.)

► Provide transportation from the nearest public transportation station, and encourage ridership (Texas Instruments and Agilent). If your municipality is planning a new public transit stop, try to get the transit authorities to put it near your company.

► Provide bicycle racks or lockers, and start a bicycle club. (Apple and TI; in Taiwan TI gives employees free bike helmets.)

► Provide preferred parking spaces for carpools. (TI, Apple)

► Offer employees who carpool a dollar a day. (Santa Monica, Apple)

► Encourage convenience stores and other services to set up shop on or near company campuses. (Compaq, Apple)

► Provide electric car recharging stations. (Apple)

► Offer free or reduced-rate mass transit passes. (IBM, Santa Monica, Agilent)

Which of these Lean and Green ideas for reducing solo commutes would work best in your organization?

(Because the RRR trilogy chapters are so closely linked, they share a single "Making It Easy" box at the end of Chapter 12.)

Chapter 11

Reuse: The Second Best Strategy
in the RRR Trilogy

We've added nothing to the landfill for eight years, except when
disposing of a plating line or tank after we've cleaned it.
— Nirmal Singh, director,
Environmental, Health, and Safety, ITT Cannon

WHEN I was in high school, a friend repeated to me what she had
learned at her Mormon Church: the Earth can support unlimited
human population growth if each family lives on and cultivates
one acre of land. I remember wondering how it would be determined which family was assigned a plot in Death Valley and
which received one in the south of France.

In reality, we humans are not equally dispersed around the
planet. Where masses of us live, our natural resources are growing scarce, landfills are choking precious land and waterways, and
air pollution from incineration and the generation and consumption of power is contributing to breathing disorders. By 2010, it is
expected that 75 percent of the U.S. population will live within 50
miles of a coastline (according to Christopher J. Evans, executive
director of the Surfrider Foundation, January 2001). This many
millions of people will not be able to share the land without
reducing, reusing, and recycling resources.

Reuse Materials to Reduce Waste and Expense

You and your organization *can* make a significant difference to the health of our planet and its inhabitants—as well as the profitability of your organization—by following some of these Lean and Green examples for *reusing* materials.

Reuse Packaging Materials At British Aerospace's machine shop, employees place freshly machined and plated titanium and aluminum aircraft-wing parts into reusable green bins that look like sturdy suitcases. While I was visiting the assembly shop late one morning, employees removed those parts from the green bins, and then the reusable packaging was rolled back to the machine shop. Danny Martland explained that any damage to an aircraft component could lead to a fracture of the jet, so it is critical to package components safely during manufacturing. Aircraft parts used to be individually wrapped in once-used packaging. Now the reusable, sturdy packaging not only provides complete protection but also reduces waste and the ongoing cost of packaging.

Ian McKeown at Polaroid began one of my favorite stories about discovering ways to reduce packaging by saying, "Anything that goes out the plant's door that isn't finished product or people is waste." When McKeown looked at what goes out the door, he saw that the biggest waste category was cardboard. Most of the cardboard being wasted was in the form of boxes that had contained piece parts shipped to Polaroid from suppliers. "We commissioned the Paper Industry Research Association to study waste reduction for us," he says. "The bottom line of the paper association's report was to recycle the cardboard." But McKeown was determined to go further: "Coincidentally, my neighbor bought a weed whacker from a German company. This particular product was new to Scotland. When I walked over to take a look, I saw lying in my neighbor's garbage can the packaging in which the weed whacker was delivered. It was made of corrugated plastic! The nearest stock of the product, Correx, was in Scotland, at Plasboard Plastics Ltd., which made boxes in which fishermen could stack polyethylene bags of ice to keep the fish fresh. It's easy material to recycle: it's a clean-base polypropylene material that's in demand now, for use in computer monitors and other high-volume products."

Today, instead of cardboard boxes, Polaroid's Scotland plant uses brightly colored Correx boxes, which are folded into shape like origami figures. Different corrugated-plastic packaging is used in different manufacturing regions, so Polaroid affixes the appropriate return labels on these reusable boxes. Because the Correx boxes are used again and again, they accumulate dust in suppliers' warehouses and in transit. "They are easy to clean with a rag and water," says McKeown; "just wipe it. The static is on the box, not on the product." When after many dozens or hundreds of uses the Correx boxes are no longer usable, Polaroid sends them back to the box manufacturer for regranulation. The granules then are formed into bins customized to serve specific functions in the manufacturing line. For example, I saw a blue box with a specialized handle for lifting and handling designed by Polaroid employees in conjunction with the box manufacturer.

At first, Polaroid's suppliers and operators used packing tape to secure the boxes. To avoid the use of unnecessary materials (the tape) and labor (applying and removing the tape), Polaroid's designers then created a superior flap that could be inserted in a slot to close the box without tape. Employees call it the "Mickey Mouse Ears" design (see diagram on next page).

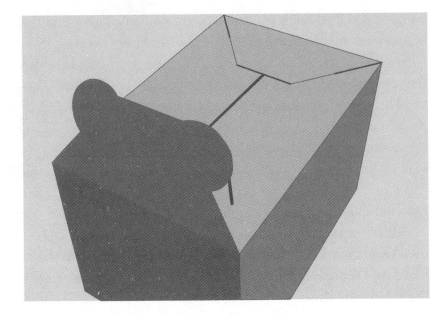

According to McKeown, "When we decided to switch from paper-cardboard boxes to Correx plastic-corrugated boxes, we knew we would save money. We've saved £3.8 million, which has exceeded our expectations." Polaroid's idea for reusing plastic-corrugated boxes has spread to other Polaroid plants and to other companies. When employees from IBM, Motorola, and Compaq saw the brightly colored Correx boxes that their suppliers were using to send parts to Polaroid, they too began using them—saving additional money for the suppliers and benefiting the environment even more. Finally, this reusable packaging may find its way into customers' hands. Although Polaroid's cameras are totally recyclable, today the final-product package is constructed of corrugated paper coated with silicon, and no recycling company wants to recycle the packaging. Ian McKeown is hoping to use corrugated-plastic for the final-product packaging; this material does not need coating, and it is sturdy and attractive enough to be used as a carrying case for the camera. The product will be labeled by wrapping a colorful paper sleeve around the corrugated plastic. The customer would keep this sturdy, lightweight box for the life of the camera and perhaps even use the case to carry other items. McKeown excitedly pointed out that this final change would mean that Polaroid would produce no waste at all.

Reuse Chemicals Of all the IBM facilities worldwide, I chose as a Lean and Green example the site in Endicott, New York, whose products—printed-circuit boards used in everything from computer printers to banking machines—traditionally have been manufactured through chemical means. Knowing that IBM was the first to certify all its facilities to ISO 14000 (the international environmental standard discussed in Chapter 6), I wanted to see how IBM treated one of its most chemical-intensive cases. Employees at IBM's Endicott site discovered a way to recover and reuse ethylene diamine tetraacetic acid, which is used plating bath that previously had to be transported for costly disposal. The process to recover the complexing agent and pretreat the remaining waste in-house was implemented for less than $750,000. In seven years, the process recovered more than 3,500 drums of chelating agent, avoided more than $1 million in raw material purchase costs, and eliminated more than $500,000 in offsite disposal transported by 750 tanker trucks containing more than 14,000 tons of chemical waste. IBM Endicott also replaced a legal chlorinated solvent with a low-volatility organic cyclic ester that can be continually reused through a closed-loop distillation process; IBM therefore needs to buy and dispose of far less of it. One gallon goes around the loop 70 times before leaving it. And because this solvent emits more than 99 percent less than its predecessor, it needs far less exhaust abatement—such as scrubbing or incineration—saving time, capital expense, and plant space. All totaled, this system has saved IBM $7 million in five years. This cost saving takes into account the $300,000 worth of energy to distill the new chemical.

Reuse Oil Oil, like other fossil fuels, is not only in limited supply on the planet, but also after its use oil easily can contribute to water and soil contamination and thus to the ill health of humans, sea creatures, and other animals and plants. Read how British Aerospace reuses oil for Lean and Green benefits. In the machine shop, where metals are cut and formed into parts of aircraft, such as components for the wings, oil is used to cool the machines. Danny Martland explains, "Now, we clean the oil of bacteria with an ultraviolet system, then reuse the oil." The benefits of this high-tech ultraviolet system go beyond doing the right thing environmentally with used oil, he says: "By removing bacteria from the oil that is reused in our machinery, we can clean our machines less frequently. If the coolant were contaminated, it would have to be wasted. So this way we don't have to pay for disposing of waste or paying for replacement oil."

Reuse Plastic One of Thomson Multimedia's recycling goals was to send less than 1 percent of the company's scrap plastic to landfill or recycling—reusing the rest of the scraps. The company achieved a reuse percentage of all but 0.7 percent. The company finds it's easier to reuse plastic that has been molded thin; thicker pieces are harder to reuse.

Reuse Water LSI Logic's Santa Clara, California, site installed two water-recycling projects in the late 1990s. One reuses process-cooling wastewater from the plant to the fume scrubbers; the other reuses fabrication-process wastewater for deionized water production. The total water savings is 64 million gallons per year—a 63 percent reduction in water usage. The return on investment is estimated to be 2.8 years.

Convincing Management and Employees to Reuse

Polaroid's Ian McKeown and his team reuse many materials—such as the boxes described above—for Lean and Green gain. To encourage you to do the same at your organization, let me tell you where McKeown's heart is when he thinks of and persuades others to use these solutions.

He loves the Leven Valley near Glasgow, Scotland. With its bonny Loch Lomond, rolling green hills, and a meandering river, who wouldn't? The Leven River draws a half-circle around Polaroid's manufacturing plant, where McKeown is the environmental manager. The evening before our day-long tour of the plant, he and his wife, Jean, took me on a tour of the countryside: we walked out onto a Loch Lomond pier and climbed up to a hilltop castle for a bird's-eye view of the valley. When McKeown talks to Polaroid's four division managers about adopting a new procedure that will save money for the company and reduce waste, he uses his engineering master's degree, his manufacturing experience, and his love of the Leven Valley. His goal is for nothing to leave his plant but people and finished product, and he's well on his way.

Chapter 12

Recycle: The Third Best Strategy
in the RRR Trilogy

> Any of our customers can send back to us anything LSI sends to
> them, including packaging materials and semiconductor chips. We
> see that these materials are easily recyclable.
>
> —Linda Gee, environmental director, LSI Logic

RECYCLING materials is great for Lean and Green—but only if
you really needed to buy the materials in the first place and can't
reuse them in their current form. Read why, from both an environmental and a business perspective, recycling is the third choice
in the RRR trilogy.

▶ **The environmental perspective** Converting a material from one
   form into another nearly always requires transportation to
   recycling facilities, energy for the conversion process, and
   more transportation to users who want the recycled materials.
   After the transformed materials are expended, they will either
   end up in landfill, be incinerated, or have to be recycled again.

▶ **The business perspective** Although organizations can earn money
   by recycling used materials, revenue from recycling is minor in
   comparison with the major cost savings achievable by reducing

unnecessary purchases and reusing necessary materials in their current form. Most small and medium-sized organizations are not earning revenues from recycling. Finally, an organization's storage, handling, and transportation costs for recycling can bite into recycling revenues.

Nonetheless, you and your organization can greatly reduce contributions to landfill and incineration by recycling materials. And I trust that after reading Chapters 10 and 11 you will be reducing the amount of material that leaves your facility and reusing most of the rest!

Recycle What You Have to Purchase and Cannot Reuse

You can recycle all kinds of materials: raw materials and finished goods, solid substances and liquids. Read on for example after example of revenue-producing recycling that otherwise would have been waste for planet and pocket.

Recycle Solid Waste The most profitable recycling scheme I found among the 20 Lean and Green organizations was at Louisiana-Pacific, which generates $26 million of revenue each year for selling by-products that otherwise would have been waste. The Hines, Oregon, facility I toured—one of the smaller mills— earns $200,000 from selling what otherwise they would have to pay to dispose of.

At Apple's Sacramento, California, facility, 97.3 percent of all incoming material is reused or recycled and therefore diverted from landfill. The revenue earned through recycling and the costs avoided by reducing waste contributed $1 million to Apple's profitability in the first year. According to Brian Rauschhuber, manager of the Americas' logistics operations, "Reducing the cost of manufacturing through reuse and recycling helps Apple to charge less for its products." Much of this success was the work of seven Apple employees who decided too much was being thrown away and formed "Team Recycle."

The European arm of Thomson Multimedia recycles 76 percent of its waste. The net cost savings from this recycling is $2 million.

Recycle Scrap during Production Chances are that your organization, while providing services or producing products, generates some scrap materials—obsolete parts, edges trimmed from products, reports comprising old data, and so forth. Here is what three Lean and Green companies do with their scraps:

▶ Polaroid recycles the small percentage of film cartridges that are used for test purposes or that break during normal manufacturing. The company hires people with physical disabilities to disassemble these film cartridges and divide the parts into metal, plastic, and film for recycling. In addition, the work gives these people some experience in industry and the chance to earn a wage.

▶ ITT Cannon earns money by selling aluminum chips and odd-shaped blocks left over from machining operations (pieces that are too small or awkwardly shaped for further extrusion, stamping, or other cookie-cutter operations). It also melts and recycles materials left over from die casting or machining steel connector shells.

▶ Inventory that is obsolete or that didn't make Compaq's quality standards have value in used computers or elsewhere in the used electronics markets. Compaq generates millions of dollars of revenue by selling these parts.

Recycle Chemicals Perseverance and creativity are at play in many chemical recycling projects. Tim Yeakley, a chemical optimization project manager at Texas Instruments, heads up the sulfuric acid recycling project, in which used chemicals are collected and sold. "We don't reuse sulfuric acid," says Yeakley. "It is not pure enough for us." Chad Mitchell, a facility system owner in Dallas, found a buyer for TI's recycled sulfuric acid, but the buyer stopped needing the chemical. So he concentrated the used sulfuric acid and found other buyers, including utility companies, machinery parts cleaners, and paper companies in Japan. Perseverance counts.

LSI Logic sells used isopropyl alcohol to a windshield-wiper company. Celestica's used alcohol goes into fuel blending. What creative applications can you think of for chemicals used by your organization?

Recycle Lead IBM found a way to recover and recycle the lead-tin alloy that was wasted during semiconductor wafer manufacturing. Lead-tin deposition in wafer manufacturing takes place in a chamber, and interchangeable shields are used to keep the overspray off the chamber surfaces. The lead-tin alloy had to be periodically chiseled off these shields, resulting in significant equipment downtime and sometimes damaged shields. A new way of protecting the shields that also enables easy removal of the lead-tin deposits was developed. The lead-tin now is peeled off the shields and collected for recycling and reuse. As a result, 8,000 gallons of lead-containing acid waste and the follow-on lead-containing rinse water were eliminated each year, and 43,700 pounds of lead-tin was recycled. This new process saves $265,000 per year in operational costs, and the increase in yield results in $3.4 million in potential revenue.

Recycle Water Mitchell's group at TI is redoubling its efforts to recycle more of the water used in semiconductor manufacturing. Its goal is to double the amount of water recycled.

Recycle Paper Paper is recycled at nearly all of the Lean and Green companies. Hisashi Sakumi at Kyocera says, "It has become a daily habit at Kyocera to recycle used paper." The company met its targets to recycle 97 percent of office paper and 100 percent of other paper; it had recycled 3,000 tons of paper, which is equivalent to about 60,000 trees.

Recycle Glass Glass beverage containers are recycled by all Lean and Green organizations, and light bulbs are recycled by many, including Agilent and Cannon. Thomson Multimedia recycles glass parts rejected during the TV manufacturing process and other glass parts such as glass "dust" collected in the dust-removal equipment.

Recycle Plastic NEC installed plastic-recycling equipment at its Sagamihara facility and a foam-plastic compactor at its Nagano site. The company now converts 600 tons of plastic waste into solid fuels and other resources each year.

Recycle Packaging Materials Kyocera earns revenues by turning recovered packaging materials into sludge and selling it to cement producers.

Recycle Food Waste NEC expanded its recycling of "canteen waste" by doubling the number of compost machines in its facilities. The installation of recycling equipment contributed to a 500-ton reduction in canteen waste, and the compost generated is distributed to local farmers. Celestica sends its cafeteria food waste from its Toronto facilities to pig farmers.

Product Take-Back A category of recycling that is getting more attention these days, owing in part to new European regulations, is "product take-back." Following a late-1990s environmental summit in Japan, the European Community signed up for a program called End of Life Electrical and Electronic Equipment. The program specifies that no part of an electrical or electronic product can go into landfill—all of the products must be recycled—and that lead will be a banned substance. Here are some examples of Lean and Green companies' emerging methods for taking back and recycling products they make:

▶ Compaq shares with customers its list of audit-approved reuse organizations, so customers can take advantage of Compaq's recycling infrastructure. And customers enjoy earning revenue from recycling, says Environmental Program Manager David Lear. "We look at it as a service to customers. In fact, we'll take back an IBM computer and sell new Compaq computers to you." Compaq's Japanese customers especially are asking for product-take-back programs.

▶ Apple takes back 600,000 pounds of product from Apple employees (primarily) and customers. To divert waste from landfill, a Cupertino, California, group earned $1 million profit by outsourcing the disassembly of returned products, selling what they could, and recycling the rest. Employees can look on an internal website to find the keyboards, hard drives, and other equipment and subassemblies they want. Corky Chew says, "We have developed an infrastructure in specific European countries to assure that our products are collected and recycled properly in accordance with national laws and prepared for the upcoming recycling directive. Apple's authorized dealers also play an instrumental role in collecting waste products."

▶ Thomson Multimedia, through French and German business associates, has arranged for the recycling of its glass computer and television screens. Michel Compérat says, "We're working with recyclers to show them the best way to dismantle our products and to improve the design of our new products for easy dismantling. We gave recyclers our specifications [to enable them to] recycle the glass, plastic, and other materials in our products. A glass recycler in France is building a new site in order to comply with our CRT glass manufacturing specifications; Thomson Multimedia will use secondary materials recycled by this new site." The new site will recycle end-of-life CRTs from computers and all brands of TV sets.

> **RESULTS OF THE RRR STRATEGY AT LSI LOGIC**
>
> ▶ **Reduce:** All employees are given ceramic mugs to avoid purchasing disposable cups, and the company's widespread use of electronic mail greatly reduces the amount of paper that must be purchased for memos, expense reports, and other documents. Money spent on paper is a fraction of what it used to be, and electronic reporting of expense reports results in faster reimbursements for employees.
>
> ▶ **Reuse:** The company used to "draw a fresh bath" each time it cleaned semiconductor parts during manufacturing. Now, the cleaning acids are reused four or five times. The company saves on purchase and disposal costs.
>
> ▶ **Recycle:** LSI recycles nearly everything it cannot reuse: semiconductor components, metal parts, packaging, white and mixed paper, computer paper, newspaper, magazines, glass, and aluminum. In many instances, money is earned through recycling.

Motivating Your Colleagues to Recycle

To help Celestica meet its goal of recycling 90 percent of its solid waste and increase recycling revenue, Ann Tenore—who heads recycling of cardboard, plastic, packaging, trays, cans, bottles, and polystyrene—labeled Celestica's waste receptacles "Landfill." It works! The company's corporate director of real estate and facilities, Jaan Meri, told me he no longer has a waste bin in his office—he uses only a communal "landfill" receptacle in rare instances.

MAKING IT EASY

Reduce, Reuse, Recycle

1. First, think of materials your organization can avoid buying in the first place. Ask yourself, "What goods and materials come into my organization's doors that end up as waste?" Promote the cost savings to your management. TI has saved multiple millions of dollars by reducing the amount of chemicals it has to purchase for "spinning" semiconductor wafers.

2. Next ask, "What, besides people and finished products, goes out of our organization's doors?" Perhaps quite a bit of the paper, packaging, and other materials can be reused.

3. Think now of the purchases you can't avoid making and the materials that cannot be reused: Challenge yourself to recycle every bit of it, even if it means changing designs or processes.

4. Finally, think about all that you recycle. Can you upgrade some of it to "reuse" or "reduce"? For example, because NEC considers it preferable to arrive at its "zero emission" goal by reusing materials rather than recycling them, employees are seeking to reuse waste oil before eventually recycling it into fuel additives.

You have saved money by reducing unnecessary purchases, reusing items you need to purchase, and recycling the rest, all of which benefit the planet.

Chapter 13

Persuade Business Partners to Be Lean and Green Allies

> We try to drive our costs down through the environmental section of our supplier rating system.
>
> —Danny Martland, environmental advisor, British Aerospace

THE Lean and Green promise that cost savings and environmental health are nearly completely compatible is based not only on steps *your* organization takes, but also on steps taken by your suppliers and the companies you acquire. Use appropriate-to-business arm twisting to get all your business partners to meet environmental specifications. Smart green practices used by your business partners can reduce *their* costs, and allow your organization to pay lower prices for those products and services.

Also, reduce the risk of being negatively associated with business partners whose practices are not Lean and Green. Partners who waste and pollute not only pass the buck—which harms your organization's reputation—but also harm the natural environment in another community or global region. And it is one planet.

In NEC's definition of a "green product," suppliers share the center stage: "The product is designed to minimize its impact on the environment throughout its life cycle, and the management of the supplier company is active in pursuing environmental protection." Harry Reid at Agilent says, "We and many of the large companies here in Scotland worry about our supply-chain management. We need to be not only socially responsible to our community, but also sure that our suppliers are responsible."

Use this chapter to get more ideas for Lean and Green step 1—question wasteful practices for Lean and Green benefit—*through your suppliers.*

How to Tell If a Supplier Is Green

Most of the Lean and Green organizations have designed a checklist that the purchasing departments send to suppliers to rate them according to green practices. NEC, for example, gathers information about the following topics in its green-product questionnaire for suppliers of parts for personal computers, cellular phones, and other personal-use products:

▶ Degree of resource conservation and energy saving incorporated into design

▶ Ease of repair and ability to extend life of product

▶ Proactive use of reused parts and recycled materials

▶ Ease of recycling

▶ Adoption of environmental management systems (independent or compliant with international standards)

▶ Implementation of product assessment

▶ Activities related to recovering and recycling used products and wrapping and packaging materials

► Activities related to preserving the ozone layer and preventing global warming

► Disclosure of information

► Use of chemical substances in products and production that are prohibited by law, those that are unacceptable to NEC, and those that can be used but require control

The responses—from more than 100 suppliers and for thousands of products—are entered into a database, so that NEC's product designers around the world can choose suppliers and products wisely.

Checking Up on Suppliers Personally Their talk may be good, but do your suppliers live up to their environmental claims? Many of the Lean and Green organizations send teams to supplier sites to verify green practices. At LSI Logic, an environmental engineer, Morgan Rider, checks up on the companies to see that they meet environmental requirements.

Due Diligence for Waste-Disposal Suppliers An organization's biggest potential environmental risk, along with the associated financial risks, may be related to waste disposal. When the U.S. Environmental Protection Agency identifies a hazardous waste site (a Superfund site), for example, the organization responsible for the pollution is charged multimillion-dollar fines and cleanup costs. You can easily convince management that company-caused pollution on this order of magnitude is caustic, not only for soil and water but also for profits!

Compaq, for example, instead of disposing of its own waste, contracts with the best vendors for waste disposal. Walt

Rosenberg advised me, "Find the best vendor to minimize the risk. Preventing one Superfund site is worth it one hundred times over."

Green Suppliers Can Create Leaner Customers

The Lean *or* Green myth includes the fallacy that environmentally sound products have to cost more. In reality, many green products cost the same as or less than their more wasteful or toxic predecessors. Many Lean and Green organizations are paying *less* to green suppliers, owing to the efficiency won through environmental practices. Diana Lyon of IBM says, "We have obtained lower prices for some materials with improved environmental attributes, such as recycled-content paper, plastic, and packaging."

But sometimes, green products *do* cost more. And this is an upside of capitalism—choose those green products that work with your organization's budget, and the law of supply and demand will do the rest. Few Lean and Green organizations say they pay more to suppliers that meet higher environmental standards if the extra cost would harm their competitive positioning. For example, NEC will not use a supplier that meets NEC's environmental protection guidelines if that supplier compromises NEC's ability to compete with other companies on price and product quality.

Your suppliers want to keep your business, and you can ask them to help you meet your Lean and Green goals. Frank O'Rourke at Celestica leaned on his suppliers to help him meet a goal of reducing his facility's $2 million chemical budget by $125,000. "This was hard to do," Frank says, "because some chemicals, such as small epoxy with specific tolerances with high-purity content, are particularly expensive given that they are custom and specific to the industry." So Frank "pushes back" on suppliers, asking them, "How can you help us to meet our reduction plan?" Frank knows that the chemical industry is quite competitive and that his suppliers want to keep Celestica's business. These suppliers are willing, therefore, to take a longer business view—looking beyond one business deal—to help Celestica meet its cost reduction goals. You too can ask your suppliers to help you be competitive and to foster a healthier environment over the long haul.

It's OK to Take a Hard Stance with Suppliers

See how these Lean and Green organizations take a firm position with suppliers: "Green up or else."

▶ LSI doesn't hesitate to change suppliers if a supplier's practices raise environmental concerns.

▶ An eco-label that Apple Computer wants to use states that its suppliers will soon be certified to the international environmental standard, ISO 14000; so Apple's agreements with suppliers require that they certify to ISO 14000 by a deadline.

▶ Ian McKeown told me that "Polaroid's vendor engineers ask suppliers, 'How do you manufacture this product?' If the suppliers use a bad substance, we'll ask them to remove it. If they don't remove it, we'll use another supplier."

Can you see yourself using such a direct approach with your suppliers? If more people did, we'd have more environmentally responsible organizations worldwide. The planet would benefit from less waste and pollution, and the businesses themselves would benefit from the reduced costs and greater revenues of the Lean and Green promise.

Nonetheless, you don't *need* to strong-arm your suppliers. Educate them about being Lean and Green for mutual benefit. Danny Martland at British Aerospace says, "We can't send our products out to a dirty manufacturer that doesn't bother with environmental standards, but we don't threaten suppliers with environmental requirements by saying, 'Do this or we won't use you.' Instead, we say, 'Here is some training to get you through the levels of environmental improvement.'" His company gives suppliers bronze, silver, or gold awards when they meet mutually agreed upon environmental improvements.

When one of Kyocera's suppliers does not meet Kyocera's standards, Kyocera sends its own environment auditors to suppliers to suggest improvements. One hundred of Kyocera's employees are now certified as ISO 14000 internal auditors, at an expense of nearly $500 each.

Whether you strong-arm, gently persuade, or educate your suppliers into becoming greener, proselytize about the profitability advantages of Lean and Green. Harry Reid at Agilent Technologies asks suppliers to develop environmental systems, and adds, "By the way, we'll send Agilent's risk manager, Ian McIntosh, to be with you for a few days to help you with your environmental management system." Reid tries to convince small companies to invest in sustainability and finds that they listen only when they are convinced of an economic benefit.

With Outsourcing, Suppliers Play a Critical Role

You may not realize that a significant percentage of the products you buy are made by companies other than the ones whose names are on the products. In the electronics industry, for example, 20 to 30 percent of products are "outsourced" to other companies for manufacturing (Technology Forecasters, Inc., *Quarterly Forum for Electronics Manufacturing Outsourcing and Supply Chain,* November, 2000, Alameda, California). The outsourcing trend can significantly affect Lean and Green processes—either positively or negatively.

Consider the company that outsources manufacturing: all the company is doing is coming up with product ideas, marketing, having shareholder meetings, and occupying an office building filled with computers and meeting rooms. A company using this business model would not normally do much damage to the environment. But that company's outsourcing suppliers could contribute either harm or benefit. *They* are the ones designing the products based on the customer's concept, buying the materials, building the products, shipping them, and repairing them. Organizations committed to being Lean and Green need to ensure that their suppliers—particularly the ones to whom they outsource major processes—are Lean and Green as well.

Ian McIntosh at Agilent said it well: "I feel that now there is so much outsourcing that it's important to focus on the environmental practices of suppliers. All companies need to study the supply chain more thoroughly. More and more the public is aware of supplier issues—and social issues too. It's an area we need to strengthen: to be more proactive in environmental reporting. We do a little bit locally, but we can do more. Our main contribution is more global—encouraging smaller companies and suppliers to be more environmentally friendly."

Checking Out Suppliers' Suppliers

When outsourcing processes, an organization needs to realize that its outside supplier may itself engage tens or hundreds of additional suppliers. How can the organization be sure that its outsource suppliers' suppliers are Lean and Green? How do you control your suppliers' suppliers? David Lear points to Compaq's five-step process, which includes what Compaq requires of suppliers' suppliers: "It's vital to ensure that suppliers' suppliers are chosen carefully. If a supplier is debarred by the U.S. government—we can't sell to the government, which is the world's largest buyer of computers."

Many of the Lean and Green organizations have been growing, both by increasing their own operations and by acquiring other companies' operations. My contacts determine that their newly acquired sites either are Lean and Green also—or are able to quickly *become* Lean and Green. David Lear at Compaq gave an example of the latter: when evaluating the potential purchase of its facility in Jaguariúna, Brazil, Compaq found soil contamination from an underground diesel tank and asbestos in the roof. Based on these negative environmental factors, Compaq negotiated a 30 percent reduction in its purchase price. The seller's corporate management was surprised about the environmental problems that Compaq's due diligence uncovered. "Compaq had more information than they did," says Lear. "Parent companies may not even know what local facilities know." Compaq insisted that the seller remove the asbestos, and Compaq initiated a voluntary bioremediation cleanup project so that today the area's soils are petroleum-free.

Frank O'Rourke has had plenty of practice conducting environmental due diligence on acquired sites; Celestica has purchased dozens of sites in only a few years' time. I like his three-phase environmental assessment: "We start with a Phase 1 assessment—a paper review of what's been on that site as far back as the records go, covering reconnoiter for drains, sewer, and the periphery." Celestica then determines whether there are leaks, spills, or contamination from anything that was on the site or whether anything in the neighborhood could have spread to the site. If Celestica plans to buy or lease-to-buy the land, the company will conduct a Phase 1 and a Phase 2 assessment; the latter involves testing the soil and ground water. Celestica also will conduct a Phase 2 assessment in a lease situation if Phase 1 suggests there might be a problem. "Phase 3 is cleanup of problems," explains Frank.

MAKING IT EASY

Enlist Business Partners to Help
Your Organization Become Lean and Green

1. Start with NEC's environmental questionnaire for suppliers at the beginning of this chapter, and modify it to fit your organization. Then, by asking prospective and current suppliers to complete your questionnaire, you'll see if they can contribute to the environmental benefits and profitability of your organization's processes and products.

2. Whenever you or your management is tempted to save money by using a supplier with a not-so-green track record, remember that your suppliers (and even *their* suppliers) can drag your organization down financially and in public opinion by making environmental mistakes.

3. Ask your suppliers for Lean and Green suggestions. Some of LSI Logic's creative environmental ideas, such as selling used isopropyl alcohol to a windshield-wiper company, come from suppliers.

4. When helping your suppliers to clean up their acts, stipulate that they pass some of the cost savings (owing to greater efficiency, reduced waste, the need for fewer permits, etc.) on to you!

Now you have the confidence that your business partners are helping — not hindering — your Lean and Green progress.

Chapter 14

Make Your Buildings More
Energy- and Cost-Efficient

Santa Monica now uses 100 percent renewable energy sources
for electricity. The cost exceeds conventional electricity sources
by approximately 5 percent, but the city has reduced electricity
use through efficiency by 12 percent, so the monetary gain is still
significant.

—Dean Kubani, senior environmental analyst,
City of Santa Monica

REGARDLESS of what product or service your organization provides, chances are that your organization leases or owns at least
one building. If that's the case, or even if you work from home,
you have lots of opportunities to make your organization Lean
and Green starting right where you sit during the workday.
According to World Watch Institute, the construction, operation,
and demolition of buildings collectively consumes up to 4 percent
of the Earth's energy and other natural resources.

Green buildings make financial sense not only because they
save money, but also because they meet ever stricter government
regulations and incentives. San Francisco is an example of a city
with a municipal code that establishes resource efficiency requirements for city-owned facilities and city leaseholds. The city
of Austin, Texas, created a green builder program, which has
worked to encourage builders in the community to take environmental measures during building design and construction.

This chapter is packed with proven ideas for achieving the

first, third, and fourth Lean and Green steps: design green buildings that reduce your organization's costs, elicit ideas from people who work in the building for making the building more efficient, and measure improvement as you go.

Let in the Light

A significant way to reduce consumption of electricity is to let a lot of natural light into the workplace. Compaq's buildings in Houston, Texas, were designed to let in natural light through skylights and floor-to-ceiling windows, thus reducing the need for electric lights. Double-glazed, high-performance glass offers ample lighting while insulating against the heat of the sun's rays. Where artificial light is necessary, Compaq uses high-efficiency light fixtures equipped with timers and motion sensors. Fluorescent tubes are removed from light fixtures where natural lighting is sufficient or where no detail work requiring bright lighting is done in the vicinity. The company has reduced expenses for light fixtures and bulbs, labor time to replace bulbs, and electricity. Environmentally, less consumption of electricity means fewer natural resources used, less pollution from electrical plants, and fewer electrical plants needed.

By switching to more energy-efficient lighting such as motion detectors and low-energy fluorescent bulbs, both LSI and Celestica have reduced their lighting costs by 30 percent. Agilent reduces lighting costs dramatically by having employees use their telephone keypads to adjust lights in their own work area according to five stages of illumination intensity. What lighting is unnecessary at your organization?

Improving Systems for Better Air—Inside and Out

It's amazing to me how much wasted energy can be avoided by fine-tuning buildings' systems. Compaq reduced its energy needs by one-third, for example, by timing the use of air-conditioning fans and adjusting the motors on the basis of building occupancy.

Texas Instruments set an aggressive goal to cut energy used per square foot of building space by 50 percent over 10 years. TI achieved a 45 percent reduction with several creative energy-saving systems, such as creating cold water or ice at night, when the demand for electricity is lower, and storing it in large tanks to use during the day to cool buildings and processes. This simple system triples the cooling efficiency, and TI receives a cash rebate from the utility companies. In fact, the utilities are now bidding for TI's power. In addition to increasing energy use efficiency, TI works with local utilities to help them generate electricity more efficiently. At one site TI built co-generation facilities, in which TI generates its own electricity and concurrently uses the heat from that process. Although the project was initially intended to fill the need for more reliable electricity, it also gave TI higher-quality power and dropped TI's net electricity expenditures by 29 percent. Mark Leypoldt, who manages TI's corporate energy program, says, "We are twice as efficient as the typical utility company because we are recovering the heat; it's a ripple effect."

Cold Climate? Warm Climate? You Can Significantly Reduce Energy and Costs

Let's start with a cold-climate example of how to reduce the cost of energy. At Agilent's campus in South Queensferry, Scotland, instead of installing cooling, heating, and other equipment on the rooftop, where exposure to cold Scottish days and nights would inhibit efficiency (and be unattractive to the surrounding community) or dedicating land to this equipment, Agilent constructed a tunnel underneath the parking lot. There it installed an underground energy center that serves the entire campus.

In the far warmer climate of Santa Monica, California, consider this innovative idea to reflect heat away from buildings to keep them cool. Light-colored surfaces on rooftops reduce the heat absorbed by buildings—and thus also the need for artificial cooling. The reflection helps reduce urban temperatures too. Santa Monica also is testing light-colored surfaces on its streets. The idea for white-top (in contrast to the blacktop normally used on streets) sprang from the Concrete Institute, and Santa Monica is the first city on the West Coast to install it on a residential street. It's stronger and thinner (only 2 inches thick) than black asphalt, reduces urban heat by 15 degrees at the street level, lasts 50 years instead of 5, and costs just a little more to install.

Creative Ways to Reduce Water Usage: Inside Your Building and Out

A down-to-earth idea is saving Agilent's South Queensferry facility 50,000 cubic meters of water each year. The urinals in the men's washrooms used to flush automatically every five minutes, 24 hours each day; needless to say, this wasted a lot of water. Now the flushing responds primarily to use, and automatic flushes are programmed less frequently. And in both the men's and the women's washrooms the amount of water used for each flush was substantially reduced.

Martin Izatt at Agilent says, "Twenty years ago, water used to be very inexpensive, so the company ran water straight through the chillers. Then in response to an increase in the price of water, we closed the loop so as not to waste water—even though this created a small cost increase in energy to run the chillers. From closing the loop, we got a return on our investment in under a year, and the water savings are still coming." According to Izatt, Agilent's employees are now coming forward with their own ideas to conserve water. "Whereas there used to be apathy about conservation ideas," he says, "now employees are more keen to be heard when they complain or volunteer an idea. This is because of personal relationships I've developed with people here. They've witnessed that when they have a good idea I'm eager to hear them, give them a pat on the back, and tell their manager."

On LSI Logic's Oregon campus, grass is planted only about 20 feet in from the roads; the rest is naturally green from the Portland area's ample rain and needs no irrigation or chemicals. Similarly, Celestica and the city of Toronto joined together to stop watering and tending some of the grounds; instead they let the existing plants grow as nature dictates. Celestica also stopped using chemicals on lawns; when weeds appear they're simply removed. To me, the grounds look tidy and professional—just slightly on the more natural side.

Surprisingly, landscaping can be designed to clean water. LSI Logic has bioswale strips in the parking lot on its Oregon campus to filter water runoff from the grounds.

Get Harmful Chemicals out of Your Building!

The city of Santa Monica is a great case study for how to remove environment- and health-damaging chemicals from your buildings, using creativity and promoting buy-in among employees. Sandra Schubert, an environmental programs analyst, describes how the city has almost eliminated the spraying of pesticides in its buildings by eliminating water sources, patching entrances, and training its employees not to store food in desk drawers. As a last resort, it uses only the least hazardous pesticides. Arriving at a pest-free environment by nearly eliminating chemicals improves workers' health, is better for the environment, and reduces the city's pest management costs by 30 percent (and monthly spraying was not nearly as effective).

Sandy Schubert also coordinates Santa Monica's toxic-use-reduction programs for the city's custodial suppliers and fleet maintenance. The custodians were using 43 different types of cleaning products—one for toilets, another for sinks, and another to polish chrome, for example. By reducing the number of cleaning products to 17 and buying them in bulk concentrated form (and thus also reducing transportation and packaging costs), the city saved 5 percent in one year. Then, alternatives to the 17 chemicals were put out to bid. Applicants were disqualified if their products were known to cause health problems, including cancer, and the products lost points if they had dyes and fragrances. "Lowest responsible bid" instead of "lowest bid" was the criterion used in choosing a winner from a dozen bidders; the latter can be an obstacle to green purchasing because green products may cost more. Suppliers were also required to ship in bulk and to use recyclable containers.

Eddie Greenberg, who oversees maintenance in Santa Monica's Promenade mall, was skeptical about alternative cleaning products. "Now," Sandy Schubert says, "Eddie is the poster child for environmentally preferable cleaners. Once, while cleaning the elevators with conventional products, he began to feel nauseous. He tried an alternative cleaner and found it to be at least as effective (if not more) as the products he had used for years, and the new product was less irritating. The city gave Eddie an award for cleanliness at the Promenade and use of environmentally preferable cleaners. He worked his way up through the ranks to supervisor. He now buys everything in 55-gallon drums with a dispenser system, using pre-labeled and -filled spray bottles."

Randall Martinez is maintenance trade supervisor for Santa Monica's public facilities. "Randall has been an ally for us," says Dean Kubani, senior environmental analyst for the city. "He takes the ball and runs with it—regarding the integrated pest-management program and phasing out all oil-based paints. He now is testing VOC-free paints. Neither Randall nor his colleagues, who also have taken off with our environmental programs, would strike me as being environmentalists. When I explain to anyone in the city, 'You can do it this way or that way, and that way is better for the environment,' they'll choose the way that's better for the environment."

Brand New Buildings Offer Brand New Lean and Green Opportunities

Building a new plant provides an exciting opportunity to employ the latest techniques in operational efficiency and waste minimization. Kyocera formed a project team to design an environmentally friendly headquarters building. The building has the world's largest vertically installed solar-energy system on an urban skyscraper, comprising 1,392 solar panels on the south wall and 504 panels on the rooftop and producing 12.5 percent of the building's energy needs. Its reduced use of petroleum results in an annual reduction of 97.2 tons of carbon dioxide in the air, 133 kilograms of sulfur dioxide, and 92 kilograms of nitrogen oxide. Now that's a "green" building you can "lean" on!

MAKING IT EASY

Green Your Buildings

1. Just start somewhere. Martin Izatt at Agilent saved his company 360 megawatt hours each year just by asking a consultant to tune the building's boiler.

2. Be willing to invest some money in your building up front for significant operational savings: LSI uses a computerized climate-control system in several of its facilities, cutting energy use in those buildings by 25 percent.

3. When your organization builds a new building, get involved at the planning stage: Danny Martland says about British Aerospace's new £80 million hanger, "It's a good idea to build the plant right — for business efficiency and the environment — from the start."

4. Your organization's property is a second "home" for your employees. By involving them in creating Lean and Green buildings you not only gather a wealth of workable ideas but also encourage green practices at their primary homes.

Your organization is doing a better job for the environment and is cutting costs by improving the quality of the air and reducing the quantity of water and energy used in its buildings.

Part III
How to Make the Most Difference

I **HAVE** shared with you dozens of cases in which the Lean *or* Green myth—the myth that businesses have to choose between focusing on the environment and being profitable—has been shattered. This old myth has been replaced by the Lean *and* Green reality: Organizational practices that are good for the environment can also be good for business.

In this, the last part of the book, I give you the *most important and quickest steps organizations can take to achieve the Lean and Green promise.* These involve putting in place the leadership and culture for becoming a Lean and Green organization.

Chapter 15

*Become an Environmental Leader
in Your Organization*

By training, educating, and empowering employees at all levels
of our organization, Louisiana-Pacific will exceed environmental
compliance standards.

—Mark Suwyn, CEO,
Louisiana-Pacific Corporation

I WANT to start the last part of this book by convincing you that
environmental leadership will contribute to creating a Lean and
Green organization more quickly than isolated actions by individuals.

Before you get frustrated and say, "But the leader of my
organization is not really interested in what's good for the environment," realize that *you* can be an environmental leader,
whether you are the head of your organization or you support
the organization in any function and at any level. As the leader, you can make Lean and Green step 3 happen: Collaborate
throughout your organization to meet Lean and Green goals.

When the Top Leader *Is* an Environmental Leader

Many of the Lean and Green organizations I visited have at their
apex organizational leaders with the environment close to their

hearts. (If this is *not* the case in *your* organization, be sure to read this chapter's next section, "When *You* Are an Environmental Leader.") Is it by coincidence or design that these leaders' organizations are truly Lean and Green? You decide, after reading these examples of environmental leaders:

▶ Key to Intel's environmental success was co-founder Gordon Moore, whom my contact Dave Stangis calls the "godfather for environment, health, and safety." Dr. Moore and his wife, Betty, gave more than $35 million of their own money to Conservation International, whose staff of scientists, economists, political scientists, and other thought leaders create ways to preserve biodiversity. Stangis says, "Gordon built in a lot of environmental thinking."

▶ In 1971, Thomas J. Watson Jr., IBM's chairman and chief executive officer at the time, established IBM's first formal environmental policy. It called for the company to be continuously on guard against adversely affecting the environment, in both process and product development.

▶ Tom Zeilinski, manager of environment, health, and safety at ITT Gilfillan, says that ITT Industry's chairman, Travis Engen, has a soft spot for the environment. "Travis believes that environment, health, and safety belong in the boardroom."

▶ NEC Corporation's president, Dr. Hisashi Kaneko, recognizes the importance of sustainability and saw to it that NEC's Eco Management Committee was chaired by a senior vice president. My Lean and Green contacts at NEC credit this environmental attention with helping NEC's subsidiaries achieve their "zero waste" target.

▶ Sony Corporation occasionally issues special editions of its employee newsletter, such as when one of its founders, Mr. Masaru Ibuka, died in 1990. Mr. Norio Ohga—then president of Sony and currently its chairman—issued a special edition to declare that Sony should reduce energy, save resources, and recycle to protect environment.

My Sony contacts said that to have a successful environmental protection program the chief executive officer has to be involved, and that without such commitment the program will not succeed. And, they said, each senior executive has to play a role in environmental protection and be accountable for that role and commitment.

You may be fortunate enough to work for or belong to an organization whose top leader is as forward thinking and convinced of the importance of the environment to business as these leaders. If you are not, I want you to know that many of the Lean and Green organizations have top leaders who excel in other areas, but not necessarily in environmental leadership. At these organizations, people throughout the ranks make a huge difference by *becoming* environmental leaders.

When *You* Are an Environmental Leader

Can a forklift operator be an environmental leader? Yes! Louisiana-Pacific's Hines, Oregon, environmental champion was a forklift operator before she applied for the job. "At first," says Lauri Travis, "I had no clue what I was doing." But now she has more than a clue; all her colleagues agree that Travis has been a great leader for the environmental programs at the facility. This site originally was being investigated as a potential Superfund site. Now it is one of only three sites to receive Oregon's

Department of Environmental Quality's coveted Green Permit, which rewards facilities that voluntarily go the extra mile to reduce environmental impacts. The program encourages companies to strive for creative solutions and systematic approaches to environmental management.

So forget the notion that environmental leaders have to be at the top of their organizations. Yes, it does help, but unless you expect to be promoted to CEO tomorrow, start today on becoming an environmental leader yourself. (*And* get this chapter of this book into the hands of your CEO.)

What is a leader? When earlier in my career I started working with leadership coach Ian Jacobsen, a fellow of the Institute of Management Consultants, I learned that a *manager* gets work done through people whereas a *leader* inspires people to meet shared goals. When visiting the 20 Lean and Green organizations, I saw far more leadership—comprising vision, communication, and accountability—than traditional management. To be the best Lean and Green leader you can be, start by giving your constituents—employees, customers, shareholders, and community—environmental vision. Communicate your vision clearly so that each employee in your organization can determine what Lean and Green action to take. Then hold employees accountable for meeting the goals they help to set.

As a leader, beware of forcing issues on people. Share with employees your environmental vision along with the Lean and Green promise; then encourage them to innovate. Nirmal Singh at ITT Cannon told me, "Environmental leadership is coaching and encouraging people at the sites, which is more effective than giving commands in a hierarchical fashion." And indeed, environmental leadership—featuring information and inspiration instead of coercion—pays off for planet and profit at ITT

Cannon. Nirmal Singh explains: "We had a tinning operation for connector contacts that required vapor degreasers. We wanted to replace the rosin so we didn't need solvents for cleaning." Because Singh believes in giving guidance rather than telling an employee what to do, he gave the responsible mechanical engineer a pep talk about starting at the source to reduce the use of chemicals. And, says Singh, "The engineer came up with an automated process that saves the company about $1 million each year."

Providing Vision: A Key Requirement of Leadership

Your organization's environmental policy statement is a statement of its vision. It also declares your stance to customers and the community and starts the process of real savings for the environment and your organization.

Introduce your environmental vision at your organization with some real-life context, both to show constituents that you care and are serious and to inspire employees to take serious Lean and Green action on their jobs. Early in the 20th century, President Theodore Roosevelt said to Americans while introducing the Antiquities Act to protect the Grand Canyon, "Leave it as it is. The ages have been at work on it, and man can only mar it. What you can do is keep it for your children, your children's children, and for all who come after you."

As a leader, work to preserve what you treasure most about the natural environment. The people you lead want you to be human—go ahead and base your environmental policy in soul as well as economics.

Before setting employees loose, give them a good view of where your organization is going environmentally and how it expects to profit. Brian Rauschhuber at Apple says, "Sometimes a group of employees has the passion to take environmental steps, but no direction. So we add focus and management to achieve incremental improvements. For example, Team Recycle got recycling up to 50 percent. And whereas the team might have been able to increase recycling on their own up to 70 or 80 percent, by putting structure and management focus around it we achieved more than 97 percent." We are talking about leadership and not dictatorship, however. Rauschhuber says, "Direction from management should not be *too* formal; for example, we would suggest replacing a shotgun approach with systematically going after first boxes, then pallets."

Still, there is a range of leadership styles at the Lean and Green organizations. The strongest approach I found was at Philips, based in the Netherlands. When I visited, Henk de Bruin reported that 150 of the approximately 250 factory units had been certified to environmental standard ISO 14000. "Our goal is to have all factories certified within 20 months. This is quite a push, and I've been stressing to Philips's Board of Management the necessity to meet this goal." The least intrusive approach I saw regarding ISO 14000 was that of Thomson Multimedia, where people at individual sites decide by themselves whether to go for certification; they are guided but not forced by the corporate group. I asked Michel Compérat how he came to believe that forcing change doesn't work as well. He replied, "Many times I've witnessed that when the company involves everyone in corporate change, such as by creating working groups for quality programs, everyone is motivated and the results always really fix the issues."

Environmental Leadership Requires Communication

It's no wonder that—after creating vision—communication is the next step for successful environmental leadership. Think of the social, political, and business leaders you admire—chances are they are excellent communicators.

An important reason I include two ITT Industries groups (Cannon and Gilfillan) in the sample of 20 Lean and Green organizations is to document how a large organization can communicate environmental vision and create synergies across its constituents worldwide. ITT gathers its North American environmental directors annually to discuss vision and strategy, has semiannual Western regional meetings, nationwide monthly teleconference meetings, and informal intra-ITT discussions. The company also brings in environmental experts from outside ITT to share the latest trends and technologies with ITT's environmental champions. These are some of the ways that your organization can "share and elevate"—as Bob Barrett of ITT Gilfillan puts it—environmental ideas and practice.

You can communicate environmental intelligence to employees in easily accessible written form as well as in meetings. Kevin Famam, Compaq's environmental program manager, tracks and disseminates environmental permits, regulation compliance, waste-minimization issues, environmental improvements in process engineering, industry trends, and other environment-related regulations and progress. "Each month," he explains, "I summarize these worldwide environmental regulations and trends in a short-and-sweet three-page document, so that the 250 people throughout Compaq who read the summary can review it on the intranet in five to ten minutes."

Communicate mistakes too! Humans make mistakes. Smart humans learn from them. Dave Stangis at Intel describes a communication program throughout the company that helps prevent the recurrence of environmental mistakes. "Existing reports were FYI and MI (management incident) reports. We created

EFYI (environmental for your information) and EMI (environmental management incident) to allow employees throughout the company to learn from incidents that have happened."

Environmental Leadership Requires Accountability

Delegating control does not mean leaving the decentralized business units totally alone and assuming that they are meeting corporate targets for environmental change. Michel Compérat at Thomson Multimedia gives an example: "I audit each European site every three years and do a follow-up audit each year. These audits are helpful not only to ensure that the sites are in compliance with regulations and company-wide standards, but also to give the sites themselves 'new eyes' to identify opportunities for improvement. After each audit, I ask the plant to create an action plan for fixing the issues during the next six months, one year, and three years. I discuss the action plan with their management. During the annual follow-up audits, I see where the sites are according to their own action plans." Compérat gives the sites points for meeting each environmental goal.

Billy Terrell, general manager of Horizon Organic's dairy in Paul, Idaho, explains that organic farming has "forced the intensity" of management: "It's an unforgiving system; we can't just treat cows with antibiotics and hormones." He says that failing to perform a procedure correctly, such as improperly attaching or detaching milking nozzles, can be fatal: "Responsibility is passed along to employees, and this fosters pride." When I asked Billy whether any employees can't handle this level of responsibility, he responded, "We've hired people we wish we wouldn't have. But most people are happy to be here."

Finding and Grooming People to Lead

Your organization has decided to delegate authority. Now you need to decide who has the knowledge and judgment to use the authority in a way that results in meeting organizational goals.

At British Aerospace's aircraft manufacturing facility, each of three plant managers nominates a champion to tackle environment issues. These nominees have a mixture of backgrounds— rarely environmental. These "environmental coordinators" are trained to recognize not only categories of manufacturing waste—general, metals, liquids, dry hazardous materials, chemicals, and recycled—but also "how our children and our children's children will be affected by the environmental choices we make today," says Danny Martland. "The environmental coordinator position is full-time now, and it's a good career move for the employee."

Shaunna Sowell of Texas Instruments says, "We shamelessly recruit employees with environmental experience from TI's internal environmental organization. Amy Anderson started out as environmental professional and now is a chemical vapor deposition (CVD) process engineer. Jennifer Sees and Lindsay Hall came to us as chemists and now are working in purchasing making sure we buy the right chemicals."

A Leader's Gravest Error: Failing to Listen to Employees

Louisiana-Pacific turned both its culture and its environmental record around—from being indicted for felony charges to winning Oregon's Green Permit. Among the employees' recommendations embraced by the new management were hiring environmental professionals for each mill, preparing for ISO 14000 certification, communicating more cooperatively with regulators, and creating a managers' handbook of environmental policy and practices. Today LP's culture is so open that all employees are trained how to talk with senior management about issues of concern. As part of Liz Smith's environmental openness tactics, she created a video for employees about LP's previous environmental indictments and the importance of reporting concerns right away. The company put a pamphlet titled "We Want to Hear from You" in the washrooms, so employees would pick them up and submit their suggestions (I noticed the pamphlets at the Hines, Oregon, mill). Several mill workers said they feel able and encouraged to make suggestions and report their concerns.

M A K I N G   I T   E A S Y

Become an Environmental Leader

1. Start with the environmental policy statement you created in Chapter 5.

2. Next, communicate the vision and give direction to employees far and wide. Create communications forums for idea sharing among employees with dedicated environmental responsibilities for sharing ideas.

3. Then, audit your organization's environmental progress. Inspiration and communication are not enough; close the loop to ensure that environmental and profitable progress are being made.

4. A good leader needs other people to lead too. Recruit high-energy environmental coordinators creatively — from universities and other companies, and from unrelated areas of your company.

Through your environmental leadership, your organization has the inspiration, direction, and follow-up needed to become Lean and Green.

Chapter 16

Work with Your Organizational Culture to Support Change

> As Intel grows, the importance of the environment snaps out at us. You better have your culture right when you're growing this fast or you'll have problems.
>
> —Larry Borgman, director,
> Environmental, Health, and Safety, Intel Corporation

EACH of the 20 Lean and Green companies has a unique company culture, just as your organization has. I witnessed repeatedly that the fastest way to make an organization Lean and Green is to adapt proven environmental steps to the existing organizational, regional, or industry culture—thereby minimizing resistance to change. Employees' messages will be heard and understood when framed in the culture known by their peers and management.

"But my organization's culture will never embrace environmental practices," some of you are thinking. As you've read so far, however, not all of the 20 Lean and Green companies were *always* Lean and Green. Cultural change can be necessary to resolve an organization's damaging practice environmentally.

In this chapter, learn how to use the best of your organization's culture—and those of your job function and geographic region—to make fast progress in Lean and Green steps 2 and 3:

Gain endorsement for Lean and Green ideas using business language, and collaborate throughout the organization to meet Lean and Green goals.

Study and Adapt to Your Organization's Culture

You may or may not love it, but your organization *does* have a culture. Study it—observe, ask your manager or co-workers about it, and look for clues in the organization's motto and procedures manuals. Notice how changes are implemented at your company. The more you know, the faster you'll be able to implement lasting Lean and Green improvements.

Now, follow in the footsteps of the Lean and Green champions by adapting your Lean and Green message to your organization's culture. Danny Martland attributes much of his environmental success at British Aerospace's Samlesbury, England, site to leveraging the company's overall culture and procedures: "The forms for environmental action in each business unit's environmental plans are kept simple; they're in a format similar to those used for standard business tasks. A failure to meet a business unit's environmental objective would be addressed during a manager's performance review—just as would a failure to meet another type of business objective."

"Look inside your organization for strong coaches, and integrate the environmental management system on that," advises Danny. "Don't bolt something foreign onto the systems you've already got. Look at how a manager runs a business review meeting, and build the environmental review around that. Tell people, 'We won't disrupt your business.' My background is manufacturing and engineering; I understand the pressures of production. And they know we do understand it, and that we're creating a simple system. We've experienced no barriers out there with this system."

In propagating your Lean and Green recommendations, pitch it within the context of your industry's culture, in addition to that of your specific organization. For example, the environmental group at semiconductor-maker Intel uses the term "best known method" (BKM)—which sounds like "known good die," a term used throughout the semiconductor industry—to disseminate environmental practices globally. New assembly and test facilities in Shanghai and Costa Rica were able to use 70 of the BKMs. The BKM concept spreads environmental ideas quickly and inspires employees to create more. Larry Borgman says, "Employees can say, 'This was my BKM, and now it's used everywhere.'"

Cultures of Geographic Regions

When bringing about organizational change, consider not only your organization's culture but also the cultures of the regions where you'd like people to adopt Lean and Green thinking. My contacts offer advice about influencing organizations region by region.

▶ In Europe, each country has its own culture as well as its own "national pursuance decree" according to European environmental regulations. Agilent's Trevor Rae compares the culture at his plant in Scotland with that of his sister plants in Germany. "The Germans are good at this because they emphasize behavior and attitudes—it's part of the German culture—plus there is a lot of legislative pressure in Germany."

▶ Holland epitomizes the distinction between most European countries and many other regions of the world: Europe has a higher-density population, fewer natural resources, and far less landfill space. Henk de Bruin at Philips says that the average person in the United States consumes six times the energy that the average person in Europe and Asia does.

▶ China presents a particular challenge for environmental change because many plants are jointly owned by local authorities, whose motivation to certify to ISO 14000, for example, is low. Yet recycling is a normal practice in China, because resources have been so scarce. Nirmal Singh at ITT Cannon says that Cannon's environmental director there sells metal left over from stamping and even collects cardboard on his bicycle: "Yet Gudy had no clue what the word 'recycling' means. To prepare for ISO 14000, all they needed to do is document what they were already doing."

▶ Environmental standards may be hardest to realize in Central and South America; Lean and Green businesses have had to intensify environmental training in Brazil, Argentina, and Costa Rica. Intel's Costa Rica plant offered a particular environmental challenge. Because of the lack of environmental infrastructure, Intel had to spend more than $1 million to treat sanitary and industrial waste. Employee awareness of environmental issues was low, so Intel's environmental engineer talks with groups of employees' parents and relatives in local hotels about the environment.

▶ In the United States environmental awareness varies greatly. My contacts at LSI Logic notice a particular environmental cognizance in Oregon. The city of Santa Monica enjoys a highly educated population to whom relaying environmental messages has been relatively easy. But even within a city cultural differences exist: the wealthiest neighborhood in Santa Monica, where the education level is at least on par with that in the rest of the city, has been the least compliant about limiting garbage disposal (instead of recycling).

Don't be afraid to play one region against another. Among ITT Cannon's numerous multinational sites, its German plant was the first to have a paperless environmental management system. In fact, the German facility's quality department had already been paperless. Its achievements inspire other ITT Cannon plants to automate their environmental management systems.

Follow on the Heels of the "Quality Culture"

In the 1970s, manufacturing strategy leaders such as Dr. W. Edwards Deming, Dr. Genichi Taguchi, and Dr. Joseph Juran aimed the corporate spotlight on something called quality. Today, looking back, we would say, "What a notion—that quality is distinct from any other aspect of manufacturing." Now, replace the word "quality" with "environmental conservation," and you will see we can further integrate the environment into every aspect of doing business.

Japanese companies' quality circles—small-group discussions among employees—received much attention several decades ago by American companies as vehicles for improving quality. Today, NEC's production facilities in Japan use small-group activities to discuss environmental issues.

Shaunna Sowell at Texas Instruments says, "For environmental accountability, we use the quality model." Has it been easier to convince employees to implement sound environmental practices than it was to improve quality in the 1980s? Two views were expressed at the conference table during my TI visit. One is that convincing employees to follow new quality procedures was harder than implementing environmental procedures, because many employees heard the message as, "You're not doing high-quality work now." The other view is that because increased quality leads to a better product, the motivation is more obvious and immediate. "To a typical worker the results of environmental programs are not as immediately or directly tied to manufacturing," says Brenda Harrison, director of Dallas's EHS services; "so we have to educate employees."

Of the 20 Lean and Green organizations, the Louisiana-Pacific Corporation underwent the most dramatic cultural shift to embrace sound environmental practices. Director of Environmental Affairs Liz Smith described the state of LP's environmental affairs in the early 1990s, before the cultural shift. Many managers viewed environmental laws with disrespect. The company had a poor relationship with many environmental regulators. When Smith first joined the company, she observed that this poor relationship was partly responsible for the regulators' increased scrutiny. Her open dialogue with regulators made more progress for the company, and she recommended to LP management that communicating cooperatively with regulators would improve relations. LP managers now understand the opportunities the environmental management system has given them and the competitive advantage in a system that ensures not only compliance but also best management and continuous improvement.

Fines were just a small part of LP's troubles at the time. The EPA charged LP with building new plants without appropriate pollution controls and fined the company $11.1 million for violations of the Clean Air Act. Then, after an LP employee in Colorado reported that management had falsified pollution-monitoring records, LP was indicted on 54 counts of felony wrongdoing, and a young mill manager was imprisoned. The EPA threatened to put all of LP (not only the Colorado site) under suspension and debarment—which they do to companies with a string of problems—that would have cost LP $150 million in lost annual revenues. The Board of Directors decided a change of management was needed. This cleared the way for an entirely new culture at LP and a remarkable turnaround.

Mark Suwyn was hired as LP's CEO in 1996. His first priority was to create an environment where people communicated honestly and openly. All 12,000 LP employees spent three to five days learning to communicate about important challenges or conflicts and how to talk with the CEO or senior management about their concerns. Liz Smith says, "LP had a 'command and control' management style. People were afraid of speaking out. This training created a learning environment by teaching employees to express ideas and share feelings and allowing them to feel safe in doing so."

Smith was able to convince the EPA, through the environmental management system she developed, to limit the suspension and debarment to the Colorado site and allow the rest of LP to rapidly adopt new environmental practices. Today, LP's commitment to a healthy environment inspires employees to become Lean and Green champions. The result is a company that is healthier than it has been in recent times in large part owing to a cultural shift that improved environmental responsibility and encouraged innovation and ingenuity.

On the day that I traveled to a remote spot in eastern Oregon to document LP's dramatic environmental turnaround, the EPA announced that it had caught LP's competitor Willamette Industries committing serious environmental infractions. Upon seeing these headlines, the LP managers I interviewed felt relieved that, owing to their company's new culture and environmental practices, LP was no longer in the news.

MAKING IT EASY

Capitalize on Culture for Lean and Green Results

1. First, characterize your organization's culture in fewer than 10 words. For example, these are the short phrases I'd use to describe several organizations' cultures: "Aim high and measure everything" (Texas Instruments); "Inspire people to volunteer" (Thomson Multimedia); "We all will achieve the highest standard" (Philips); "Educate people and they'll choose the right thing" (Santa Monica); "Follow the corporate dream and beliefs" (Horizon Organic Dairy).

2. Even if your organization's culture is, as Liz Smith described the *old* Louisiana-Pacific, "command and control" style, use that culture to bring about change. Convince the top of the organization of the fiscal benefits of your well thought out Lean and Green ideas. Emphasize the costly risks of ignoring these ideas, without criticizing anyone. Point to the profitable turnarounds at Louisiana-Pacific, in Santa Monica, and in other Lean and Green organizations. The ride may be turbulent; hang on to your hat.

3. Consider next how your company introduced other changes, like a quality program or new business structure. Who approved the final plans? How was the information disseminated to employees? How were results measured and corrected?

4. Finally, frame your Lean and Green ideas in ways that fit your company's culture, and implement changes in ways that have worked for your company before.

Your organization will perceive your Lean and Green changes as being in harmony with the organization, and both managers and employees will more readily do their parts.

Chapter 17

Be an Environmental Activist
Using Tactics That Benefit *Business*

> I continually challenge the norm. People would say that the vast
> number of changes here is not because of my intellectual or tech-
> nical impetus, but because I challenge people at the forefront.
>
> —Harry Reid, facilities manager, Agilent Technologies

AN ACTIVIST is someone who takes positive, direct action to achieve a goal. You can apply your talents to becoming an environmental activist whose tactics are good for business, as these people did:

► At Apple Computer, seven upstart employees felt that their company could recycle more. They formed a group they called Team Recycle. On their own and in only one year, they increased Apple's Sacramento facility's recycling stream to 50 percent; now recycling is up to 97.3 percent. The money saved is nearly as dramatic.

► Kath Hindle, an administrative assistant at British Aerospace, runs an at-home environmental education program for employees that includes a shopping quiz they can use when they purchase items for themselves. She is taking the Lean and

Green promise for environmental good and money savings beyond her company's walls.

In this chapter, learn how presenting a business case with conviction is the best way to activate Lean and Green practices in your organization, and how using language that management respects is far more effective than using detraction tactics. You'll make significant progress along steps 1 and 2: Question wasteful practices and gain endorsement for Lean and Green ideas using business language.

Tactics Used by Lean and Green Activists

At your organization you may need to use business-appropriate scare tactics to sell environmental ideas to management. Some of the following tactics from the Lean and Green champions may fit your organization's situation beautifully; others may inspire you to create tactics that work where you work.

Lead with the "Lean" Part of Lean and Green The first guideline for environmental activists is to stress to management that your idea will allow the organization to become leaner—more profitable. This case was easy for Apple's Team Recycle to make because of the obvious cost benefits from reducing waste and earning revenue through recycling. Leading with the lean argument works even when the monetary returns are not as obvious.

Plant Seeds and Water Them Liz Smith at Louisiana-Pacific uses a "plant the seed" technique with her senior management. She'll say, "Here is an idea for reducing environmental impact and saving money." The facts and figures she presents to senior managers spell out how the ideas relate to their short- and long-term goals. Because the ideas are out there—repeated and made available—they get used.

If at First You Don't Succeed . . . Ian McKeown at Polaroid at first received a no to many of his Lean and Green ideas. His most effective technique to get to yes is persistence: repeatedly asking seemingly innocent questions about current procedures and showing people the benefit of environmental ideas. To overcome people's resistance to trying new processes that will benefit the environment, McKeown espouses the Japanese practice "Ask Why Five Times." He finds that although people may first respond defensively when asked why or why not, gradually they lose their defensiveness and become open to an idea. McKeown says it took Polaroid's U.S. facilities a while before they adopted the corrugated-plastic take-back idea that in Scotland had successfully reduced waste and cost. I asked him how the U.S. Polaroid employees were finally convinced to adopt the idea. "Some managers from the U.S. warehouse group were visiting Scotland for various meetings," he said. "I grabbed them and showed them the idea. And they said, 'Why don't we try it?'" Polaroid's idea for reusing plastic-corrugated boxes has spread not only to other Polaroid plants, but also to other companies. When visiting some of the same suppliers that Polaroid uses, employees from IBM, Motorola, and Compaq saw the brightly colored Correx boxes containing piece parts on their way to Polaroid. Now many of these other companies use and reuse Correx boxes—saving additional money for the suppliers and benefiting the environment even more.

Be Willing to Play Politics My favorite of McKeown's persuasion techniques is the one he used to persuade the film division's management and operators to use clearly labeled and color-specific recycling bins (which are made from regranulated retired Correx boxes). The operators, after testing the quality of the film at certain stages of manufacturing, used to drop the scrap—film, plastic, and metal parts—into the trash. Management at first rejected his idea for separating and recycling the scraps. They claimed that the operators would not want to use the recycling bins. Knowing that there was a dispute at the time between management and the operators, McKeown said to the operators, "Management told me that you wouldn't want to use the bins." That clinched it—the operators agreed to use the bins (in part, perhaps, to spite management). Ian told me, "You use what you can and most of the time it's easy, as people do want to do a good job."

Begin with Your Example Linda Gee at LSI Logic told me during lunch that she uses the same alarm clock she was using in college and drives a fuel-efficient 1984 car. At work, she reuses booties when entering her reduced-static manufacturing building. This and many other steps Gee takes save her company money *and* improve the planet—and set a good example for others as well. Liz Moyer at Texas Instruments says she is a poster child for telecommuting. Because her home is approximately an hour's commute by car, she works from her home office a few days each week to save time, reduce commuting costs, and avoid fuel consumption and pollution. Moyer personally attests that management is quite supportive of this environmentally beneficial employee practice.

Be One Step Ahead of Objections I pressed Danny Martland at British Aerospace into admitting that *some* barriers have come up when he and the environmental coordinators seek to influence manufacturing to make Lean and Green improvements: "The exception is people who have production pressures and problems, so in these cases we do have to support, advise, and facilitate. We always want to be one step ahead, such as explaining the role of the environmental coordinator. And if they say, 'I don't have any-one who is trained to be an environmental coordinator,' I'm pre-pared to say, 'I have a training course ready.'"

You Don't Have to Be an Expert — Just Ask Lots of Questions Lest you get intimidated by these successful Lean and Green activists, real-ize that you don't have to be an expert in either environmental or business processes to create and implement effective ideas. Bill Zehnder at ITT Gilfillan, for example, is not a chemical expert, but nonetheless he earned the ITT Defense & Electronics President's EHS award for replacing chemical-intensive stencil-ing and cleaning with a chemical-free solution that is quicker, less expensive, and eliminates toxic waste. In designing the new processes, Zehnder had to make some environmental choices, such as using crushed walnut shells as the cleaning abrasive instead of sand because sand contains crystalline silica. How did he know what to use? Zehnder's colleagues say that he has a hands-on approach and asks questions until he *becomes* an expert.

Career Benefits of Being an Environmental Activist

Trying your hand as a Lean and Green activist can be good for your organization and the environment, and also for your career. For example, you might become an environmental auditor: NEC and Sony each hold seminars to train employees as environmen-tal auditors, and each company has a large and growing base of auditors worldwide. You also might use the business-savvy skills

you developed in making your Lean and Green cases to get promoted within your organization. At Compaq, says Walt Rosenberg, "Staff members use their environmental experience to
move up in different parts of the company, or move up in this
group. We offer access to operations and functions worldwide—
everything is open to them."

Most of the successful Lean and Green activists I interviewed
for this book came to their positions by happenstance. Can you
see yourself in any of their personal stories? `

Nirmal Singh, head Lean and Green guru at ITT Cannon, was
born and raised in Berkeley, California. Being an outdoors person,
he decided in college that he wanted to work in the environmental field. He stressed that he wanted to approach it from a technical standpoint, such as by studying chemicals.

Danny Martland, who has been working at British Aerospace
for 20 years, appreciates the countryside and likes to fish. "My
background was in engineering, manufacturing, and occupational
health and safety," he explains; "but when it was time for our
company to prepare for ISO 14000 certification, I was chosen as
the overall champion." When I asked Danny how he summoned
the confidence to lead British Aerospace in certifying its first
facility, he responded, "I was prepared to take on the challenge, I
guess; I thought it would be a good career move, and indeed it has
been."

Several years before joining Louisiana-Pacific, Liz Smith was
widowed. With her children in school and doing well, she decided
to invest in her own future and begin a challenging career in the
environmental field, which gels with Liz's philosophy and personal interests: she raised organic vegetables, went backpacking,
and her late husband was a wildlife biologist. It was while she
was earning her degree in environmental resources engineering

and working as an energy analyst for Pacific Gas & Electric that she saw the advantages of working in industry: "The opportunities are greater [than in consulting or government], results grander, and I can see the fruits of my labor from start to finish—all the while making a big improvement for industry by helping management to see that environmental steps are profitable in many ways."

"I wouldn't classify myself as a Greenie," says Ian McIntosh at Agilent. He has a chemical engineering background, of which environmental management is a huge part. He had been heading up engineering operations for the company's printed-circuit-board plant, now closed. "At that time," he says. "I made a natural transition to the environmental management group. I understand the technologies that are available and the business climate and understand the big picture. I like to do things that are closer to Earth."

Frank O'Rourke at Celestica started in zoology, thinking he wanted to be a veterinarian. It was difficult program, however, and he chose not to pursue it. After talking with a friend who was chief lab manager at a London hospital, Frank got the idea to talk to a guidance counselor who suggested industrial hygiene. "So I gave it a try and realized, 'Wow this is great! It's science *and* a helping profession.' I'm here to protect the health and safety of our workers and to protect our environment." He obtained a degree in environmental studies and a diploma in industrial hygiene, which covers chemicals, toxicology, how chemicals are used, and their impact on operators' health.

MAKING IT EASY

Become a Lean and Green Activist

1. If you have time to read only one sentence in this chapter, read this one (from the second page): The first guideline for environmental activists is to stress to management that your idea will allow the organization to become leaner — more profitable.

2. Then, set aside any hesitation about presenting your Lean and Green ideas to your organization. In fact, some Lean and Green tactics are fun. A security guard named Noriko Takagi at the Texas Instruments site in Miho, Japan, made an origami swan from recycled office paper. She thought of this idea herself to encourage her fellow employees to recycle.

3. Consider your career goals with the environment in mind. Just as people in technology have been highly employable in recent decades, people who have demonstrated business-savvy environmental success are starting to be high in demand.

4. Finally, if you are feeling discouraged by your initial attempts to convince management, stoke your own environmental fire and try again. Three Lean and Green champions volunteered to me that their children remind them of their obligation to leave a better planet. Also mentioned as inspiring the champions were Rachel Carson, who wrote the 1962 book *Silent Spring*, and Ray C. Anderson, author of *Mid-Course Correction*.

You can channel your efforts toward taking positive, direct action to achieve environmental *and* business goals. You are an environmental activist!

Chapter 18

The Fastest Route to Lean and Green

First, stop thinking of "the environment" and "profitability" as two separate entities. For a company to be successful you have to stop the divisiveness. They automatically marry.

—Bill Brunson, facilities manager, Apple Computer

YOU'VE read more than a hundred Lean and Green success stories, chronicling environmental steps taken by organizations ranging from dairies to semiconductor companies and resulting in millions of dollars of savings and earnings. Now, where do *you* start at your workplace and other organizations you'd like to influence? As you read this last chapter, let the Lean and Green champions inspire you one last time to do all you can for the success of your organization and a healthy, thriving natural environment.

Bottom-Line Words of Wisdom from Lean and Green Champions

Let's give our Lean and Green champions some final words about how we can make our organizations Lean and Green. Notice that woven throughout their recommendations are all four Lean and Green steps.

The Four Lean and Green Steps

1. Question wasteful practices, and design Lean and Green steps to benefit profit and planet.
2. Gain endorsement for Lean and Green ideas using business language.
3. Collaborate throughout the organization to meet Lean and Green goals.
4. Measure your organization's Lean and Green progress, and strive continuously to improve.

IBM's Diana Lyon summarizes four main strategies for green and profitable solutions:

1. Commit to excellence in all areas of business.

2. Align and integrate environmental and business objectives.

3. Proactively anticipate issues.

4. Take voluntary actions to implement projects that are good for the environment and good for business.

Diana now gives us, conversely, four ways to *harm* the bottom line:

1. Being fined for noncompliance.

2. Being forced to implement mandatory government programs owing to underperformance.

3. Earning a negative corporate image that affects a company's ability to be on a bidder's list, thus losing potential revenue.

4. Paying costs associated with remediation resulting from inadequate environmental protection.

Linda Gee at LSI Logic advises, "Go for the low hanging fruit first. Companies can save real money by reducing raw material, energy, and water usage—and get positive environmental results at the same time. Over time, however, responsible organizations need to buy that ladder to reach those higher environmental goals; this demonstrates that they are in business for the long haul. For LSI Logic, maximizing yields, optimizing material usage, and reducing waste has resulted in lower production costs and pollution prevention. The way you save money is by avoiding manufacturing steps. Use chemicals more efficiently or find ways to reuse them." As two examples, LSI cut by four-fifths the amount of acid used to "bathe" chips, and the company recycles solvents on-site for repeat use.

I asked Polaroid's Ian McKeown where he started in his waste-reduction efforts, to reach Polaroid's goal of reducing waste by 50 percent in only five years. He said his methodology for environmental management can be reduced to these three points:

1. Measure what you have.

2. Start improving from there.

3. Focus on the 20 percent of the issues that are causing 80 percent of the problems.

Martin Izatt, building program development manager at Agilent, sets these priorities for conservation: first, electricity; second, water; and third, gas. Why? Because in years past the South Queensferry facility spent, annually, £600,000 for electricity, £90,000 for water, and £60,000 for gas. Izatt started with strategies that would yield the highest rewards to profit and planet.

Thomson Multimedia's Michel Compérat names the two most important steps on the road to becoming Lean and Green: "Landfill avoidance is the most important. Out of all the steps that can be taken, we favor upstream measures such as designing products in a way that minimizes waste production throughout the manufacturing processes. This may occasionally mean designing out substances, as when we decided to skip the painting stage when manufacturing TV cabinets."

Sony prioritizes its environmental programs according to the most urgent ecological issues—global warming, loss of the ozone layer, the reduction of wasted materials, and controlling the release of pollutants into the environment—effectively and systematically. And by taking some of these steps, Sony saves money: The company saved more than $3 million in the United States alone by reducing electricity and industrial waste (36,000 tons of industrial wastes including PC boards and office paper).

Danny Martland at British Aerospace says, "Of everything we've done, the employee suggestion program has reduced environmental impact the most. Last year alone through employee ideas, we reduced general waste by 17 percent and our recycling has increased 225 percent; recycled materials reached 252 tons. All of this employee-originated environmental improvement is on the background of a site that's getting busier and busier; we've added a thousand people and still we are making environmental improvements."

Is This Enough for the Planet?

As I conducted my Lean and Green research around the world and wrote this book, one question gnawed at me: Are the Lean and Green organizations I studied doing enough to reverse the course of environmental destruction on the planet? Quite honestly, I think the answer is no.

To see how they weighed in on the question, I asked the 20 Lean and Green champions directly, "Is all that your organization is doing enough for the environment?" Here are 6 of the 20 "no" responses I received:

▶ "When we have zero impact on the environment, that will be enough." (Liz Moyer, Texas Instruments)

▶ "We are doing a lot, but it's not enough. Or perhaps we're starting to work on this subject a little too late. It's better to act on a global scale, instead of being happy when one transfers environmental problems to another country or media. The French writer Saint-Exupéry wrote that the Earth is not a heritage from our parents; we just borrow it from our children." (Michel Compérat, Thomson Multimedia)

▶ "When we look at what we can do today, we are doing enough. In ten years we'll look back and say, 'If we'd only known we could have done more. If we'd only seen it sooner,' such as focusing on environmentally sound products, rather than only on process." (Walt Rosenberg, Compaq)

▶ "Even though we are using less water here than if the land stayed a farm or dairy, or if it were a typical semiconductor fabrication plant, you can't ever say you're doing enough in terms of conserving water." (Dave Stangis, Intel)

▶ "Global warming will affect us this century. The ocean current—responsible for maintaining fishing grounds, transportation, and climate—could break down and reverse owing to changes in water temperatures. Over decades Earth's habitats will adjust, but we will experience economic crises, which will force people other than early adopters to change." (Dean Kubani, Santa Monica)

▶ "We have three choices for our future: (1) Boiled frog—The planet will spiral downward as each country acts without looking at global issues, like a frog that doesn't think to jump out of water slowly coming to a boil until too late. (2) Geopolitics—Supranational governmental bodies will become powerful and lead the world in a survival mode, drastically limiting freedom of movement for people and companies. (3) Jazz—We first agree on a scheme to save the planet, then although everyone plays his or her own part, to the outside audience it sounds great. We in business have polluted the planet for the past 25 years, and we are the only ones who really can solve the problem. In a society that buys products, travels, and consumes fuel, business is always involved. So the businesses can come up with solutions." (Henk de Bruin, Philips)

So if the Lean and Green practices of the world's organizations are not enough to stem the tide of environmental breakdown, what more can be done? Here are some important ways you and your organization can go further.

Influencing Green Behavior at Home Another compelling reason for organizations to adopt Lean and Green behavior is to more quickly influence their employees' behavior at home. Bill Brunson at Apple told me, "Employees have a lot of pride in the percentage of materials recycled at Apple. We hope that people on the shop floor take these good practices home with them. We hope that if some of our employees own houses in the development across the street, that their environmental practices will be better than their neighbors' practices."

Achieving Sustainability Several of the Lean and Green visionaries look to the concept of "sustainability" to guide organizations in truly doing enough to restore and protect the planet. "The next environmental hurdle," said Walt Rosenberg at Compaq, after we'd been discussing environmental standard ISO 14000, "will be sustainable development, which will be key in our industry. Today we need to determine what this means and how to marry it with our market; timing is key."

Barney Little at Horizon Organic Dairy says that sustainable agriculture is possible. It yields no waste, cartons and containers are reused, office paper is recycled—it's a closed system. He notes, "If everyone were doing it, there would be no landfills." Santa Monica's guiding principles are in line with The Natural Steps Framework (see sidebar). Dean Kubani explains, "ISO 14000 says how to use resources and generate waste more efficiently—helping organizations to drive toward the cliff more slowly."

> **The Natural Step**
>
> The Natural Step is a nonprofit environmental education organization working to build an ecologically and economically sustainable society. It offers a framework that is based on science and serves as a compass for businesses, communities, academia, government entities, and individuals working to redesign their activities to become more sustainable. The Natural Step Framework holds that in a sustainable society, nature won't be subject to systematically increasing:
>
> 1. Concentrations of substances extracted from the Earth's crust;
> 2. Concentrations of substances produced by society;
> 3. Degradation by physical means; and, in that society,
> 4. Human needs are met worldwide.
>
> Their web site is www.naturalstep.org.

Agilent's Harry Reid says, "For too many years ours and other large companies didn't realize that the world is not only human real estate but it belongs to all creation." He remembers that until recently standard corporate grounds were well-manicured gardens with nothing natural left, just short grass, fountains, and trees: "I used to be like this but I've had my head bashed about a number of things. Sometimes you have to say, 'Let's let that part grow wild and be as it is, because a butterfly can form a habitat there.'" Harry Reid took this symbolic step toward sustainability: he converted a section of parking lot into a wildlife garden, which is home to native Scottish flora and fauna and an occasional visiting place for employees; the setting is so lovely and relaxing that many employees and their managers go to the garden for performance reviews.

Improving the "Social" Environment   Harry Reid at Agilent in Scotland and Dean Kubani in Santa Monica, California, agree that sustainability has to grow beyond being a middle-class notion. "One fellow I know," says Reid, "lives in a drug area in Glasgow. He said, 'Don't ask me to pick up trash around my grounds when I could get poked with a hypodermic needle.' When it's a middle-class issue only, we're missing out on millions of people. We've got to work not only to save the planet for our children, but also to educate them into seeing the reason why." In Santa Monica, Kubani has heard citizens say during an affordable housing conference that safety concerns come ahead of environmental concerns. They say they don't want landscaping because people can hide behind it; instead they want big locking gates and bulletproof windows. Dean says, "You have to make the community a safer place before citizens will worry about the environment. That's why the upper middle class is most concerned; we don't have to worry about getting shot."

Upend the Whole System or Pace Yourself?

We now know the fastest route to Lean and Green, and yet we also know that even the Lean and Green champions profiled in this book believe they are not doing enough for the planet. So, what exactly is our task?

Danny Martland at British Aerospace makes a distinction between big-picture evaluations of wide practices—such as the environmental impact of air travel compared to other travel—

and courses of action that yield immediate environmental improvements. "Initially we got involved in the big-picture type of debate," he says; "but when you delve into it too deeply it becomes a monster and you can't manage it. We do have a materials and a development department that looks this far ahead; they look for alternatives to cadmium, review upcoming legislation, and predict what routes we might be pushed down."

Put another way,

> "It is not upon you to complete the task, but neither are you free to desist from it." (Rabbi Tarfon, Pirkei Avot, the Talmud)

I wish you success with all of your Lean and Green efforts—both for the bottom-line growth and profitability of your organization and for the benefit of the planet.

Glossary

£ British pound. 1 British pound = 1.479 U.S. dollars (December 20, 2000)

Canadian dollar 1 Canadian dollar = 0.661 U.S. dollars (January 24, 2001)

carbon dioxide Odorless, colorless natural gas in the atmosphere and in water. The most serious greenhouse gas, because of the large amounts created by human activities. With air and moisture, CO_2 forms carbonic acid, which can eat away at buildings; see Geoffrey C. Saign, *Green Essentials* (San Francisco: Mercury House, 1994).

CE mark An eco-label that certifies that a product conforms to standards concerning electrical interference, safety, design, materials, and other factors in addition to environmental ones.

CFC Chlorofluorocarbon, a substance that contributes to ozone thinning

Dutch guilder 1 Dutch guilder = .4124 U.S. dollars (December 20, 2000)

eco-label An eco-label generally certifies (through a government agency, industry group, or specific organization) that a product performs with minimal negative impact on the environment. Eco-labels signify that a product meets the environmental attributes specific to that label.

HCFC Hydrochlorofluorocarbon, a substance that contributes to ozone thinning and also is categorized as a "greenhouse gas"

ISO 14000 ISO stands for the International Standards Organization, which created standards for organizations' quality, environmental, and other practices. The number 14000 designates an environmental management system being adopted by organizations around the world. Independent firms certify organizations according to ISO 14000 when these organizations demonstrate that their environmental management systems meet the standards.

net present value Amount needed for investment today at current interest rates to have a specified amount of money at a specified time in the future (months, years). The value of cash to be received in the future expressed in today's currency.

polyvinyl chloride (PVC) Petrochemical formed from the toxic gas vinyl chloride (VC), used as the base to create plastic. Production and burning of PVC can lead to formation of toxic chemicals such as dioxins; see Geoffrey C. Saign, *Green Essentials* (San Francisco: Mercury House, 1994).

profit The result of subtracting all expenses from revenue

semiconductor pin One of tens or hundreds of pins, or metal "legs," that connect the semiconductor to the rest of the electronic device

Superfund A program of the U.S. Environmental Protection Agency established by the U.S. Congress in 1980. The EPA established methods for identifying hazardous waste sites, selecting cleanup remedies, and restoring the locations to productive use. By September 2000, the

EPA had completed construction and cleanup at more than 750 sites. Multimillion-dollar fines and cleanup costs are assigned to the organization responsible for the pollution. For more information, go to www.epa.gov/superfund.

wafer **(semiconductor wafer)** Thin round slice of pure silicon, cut to make semiconductors. Silicon, the primary ingredient of beach sand, is a semiconductor of electricity.

yen 1 yen = 0.00846 U.S. dollars (January 24, 2001)

Index

A

Accountability, importance of, 40, 174

Accounting methods, 63–65

Acquisitions, 89, 147, 154–55

Activists
becoming, 194
career benefits of being, 191–93
defined, 187
examples of, 187–88, 192–93
tactics used by, 188–91

Agilent Technologies, 4
activists at, 187
environmental management system of, 83–84
environmental policy of, 73
green buildings and, 26, 30, 159–60, 160–61, 164
profitability of environmental steps at, 36
recycling materials at, 141
reducing consumption at, 4, 36, 127, 197
regional culture and, 181
suppliers and, 148, 152, 153

Airbus, 104

Air pollution, 53, 88, 126, 127

Anderson, Amy, 175

Anderson, Ray C., 194

Annapolis, Maryland, 5

Apple Computer Corporation, 4
activists at, 187, 188
customers' expectations and, 91, 93
employee involvement at, 49–50, 200
environmental leadership at, 171–72
environmental management system of, 82–83, 86–87

Apple Computer Corp. *(continued)*
  environmental policy of, 32–33, 76
  recycling materials at, 4, 13, 37,
       138–39, 142–43, 187, 188
  reducing consumption at, 127
  suppliers and, 151
  tracking environmental progress
       at, 58
Asia, customers' expectations in, 93
Audits, 65–66, 174, 191
Austin, Texas, 157
Automobiles, pollution from, 126–27

B
Barrett, Bob, 14, 26, 111, 112–13, 173
"Before and after" stories, 15–16
Blue Angel eco-label, 96–97, 102
Boeblingen, Germany, 26, 36
Boeing, 104
Bonuses, 48–50
Booth, Mac, 44
Borgman, Larry, 51–52, 179
Boulogne, France, 8
Boycotts, 39
British Aerospace, 4
  activists at, 187–88
  employee involvement at, 4, 24, 198
  environmental leadership at, 175
  environmental management
       system of, 46–47
  green buildings and, 164
  green products of, 104
  organizational culture of, 180
  reducing consumption at, 10, 13–14
  reusing materials at, 130, 134
  suppliers and, 152
  tracking environmental progress
       at, 59
Brunson, Bill, 37, 50, 76, 87, 195, 200
Buildings, 157–64
  lighting, 158
  new, 163, 164
  reducing energy costs for, 158–60
  reducing water usage for, 160–61
  removing chemicals from, 161–63
Business language, using, 31–42

C
California Circuits Association, 92
Canada, customers' expectations in,
       94
Carbon dioxide, 2
Carcinogens, eliminating, 37, 40, 124
Carpooling, 127
Carson, Rachel, 194
Case studies, negative, 52–53
Celestica Inc., 4
  acquisitions and, 154–55
  customers' expectations and, 95–96
  employee involvement at, 50–51
  green buildings and, 158, 161
  profitability of environmental
       steps at, 35
  recycling materials at, 105, 140,
       142, 143–44
  reducing consumption at, 4, 13-14,
       35, 125
  suppliers and, 150–51
  tracking environmental progress
       at, 62
Chandler, Arizona, 5
Chemicals
  recycling, 140
  reducing, 123–24, 161–63
  reusing, 133–34
Chew, Corky, 91, 93
China, 182
Chlorofluorocarbons (CFCs), 9, 36,
       40–41, 125
Clean Air Act, 124, 184
Cleanup, savings in, 16, 110, 149–50
Coalition for Clean Air, 53

Collaboration
  outside your organization, 26, 52–54
  throughout your organization, 26, 43–52, 55
Communication, importance of, 172–74
Commuting, 127–28
Compaq Computer Corporation, 4
  acquisitions and, 154
  customers' expectations and, 92, 94, 96, 106
  eco-labels and, 96
  employee involvement at, 26, 47, 48, 192
  environmental leadership at, 173
  green buildings and, 158, 159
  recycling materials at, 139, 142
  reducing consumption at, 4, 127
  reusing materials at, 14, 132, 189
  suppliers and, 149–50, 154
  tracking environmental progress at, 57, 65–66
Compérat, Michel, 27, 64, 72, 77, 84–85, 87, 97, 109, 143, 174, 197–98, 199
Competitive spirit, appealing to, 41
Competitors
  exchanging green ideas with, 26
  getting an edge on, 13–15, 92, 98, 99, 102
Conservation International, 168
Cooling, saving on, 35, 36
Correx boxes, 131–32, 189
Corrigan, Wilfred, 10
Costa Rica, 94, 181, 182
Creativity, using your, 21, 27–29, 30
Customers
  eco-labels for, 93, 96–98

environmental expectations of, 91–95, 99
  training, in green practices, 95–96

D
Dallas, Texas, 8, 76, 140, 184
De Bruin, Henk, 22–23, 31, 41, 63, 67, 73, 74–75, 103, 120, 172, 181–82, 200
Decentralized approach, 46–47, 55, 84, 174
Deming, W. Edwards, 183
Design, 89, 109–17
  of processes, 110–13, 117
  of products, 113–15, 117
Designers, training, 115–16
Detractor, avoiding being a, 32, 38–41, 66
Dionne, Edan, 35, 86
Dolan, Steve, 26
Droms, William G., 42
Dumbarton, Scotland, 7

E
Eco-labels, 93, 96–98
ECOSYS printer, 102, 104
EcoVision, 41, 50, 63, 67
Eindhoven, Holland, 7
Electricity. *See* Energy
Emergency preparations, 87, 88
Employees
  behavior of, at home, 200
  commuting, 127–28
  convincing, to recycle, 143–44
  convincing, to reuse, 135
  empowering, 46–47
  listening to, 175–76
  motivating, 48–51, 77–78
  wasteful practices questioned by, 22–24
Endicott, New York, 5, 123, 133

"End of Life Electrical and Electronic Equipment" directive, 124–25, 142

Energy conservation, 9, 61, 88, 113–

Energy conservation *(continued)* 14, 115, 121, 158–60. *See also* Gas; Oil

Energy Star, 93, 96, 97

Engen, Travis, 168

Environmental leadership
accountability and, 174
communication and, 172–74
finding and grooming people for, 175
listening to employees, 175–76
at the top, 167–69
vision and, 171–72
you and, 169–71, 177

Environmental management system
creating, 83–85, 90
defined, 82–83
emergencies and, 87
example of, 87–89
importance of, 81–82
pitfalls for, 85–87

Environmental policy
examples of, 77
importance of, 71
using, 76–78
writing, 72–76, 79

Environmental progress, tracking, 57–68

Ericsson, 73

Europe
customers' expectations in, 93
"End of Life Electrical and Electronic Equipment" directive, 124–25, 142
regional culture of, 181

European Association of Consumer Electronic Manufacturers, 97

Evans, Christopher J., 129

Example, setting an, 190

Exxon, 53, 94

Exxon Valdez, 52–53

F

Fairchild, 10

Famam, Kevin, 65, 173

Fines, savings in, 16, 38, 110, 149–50

Food waste, 141–42

G

Gas, 60, 126–28. *See also* Energy; Oil

Gauss, Werner, 26, 30, 36

Gee, Linda, 10–11, 28, 45, 77, 85, 87, 92, 137, 190, 196–97

Germany
Blue Angel eco-label, 96–97, 102
culture of, 181

Glass, 141

Global warming, 61, 112, 199

Gowen, Paul, 71, 72, 74, 77–78

Greenberg, Eddie, 162

GreenChip, 13, 103, 113–15

Green products
areas for enhancing environmental performance, 73
designing, 113–15
eco-labels for, 93, 96–98
increased revenues from, 10, 13, 102–5
suppliers and, 147–48
true cost of, 101, 104

Gresham, Oregon, 6

H

Hall, Lindsay, 175

Harrison, Brenda, 76, 184

Hazardous material storage, 88

Hazardous waste management, 8, 9, 88

Helms, Bob, 115
Hewlett-Packard. *See* Agilent
    Technologies
High-tech industry, 95
Hindle, Kath, 187–88
Hines, Oregon, 6, 138, 169, 176
Horizon Organic Dairy, Inc., 5
    environmental leadership at, 174
    green products of, 10, 102
    reducing consumption at, 5, 119
    tracking environmental progress
        at, 66–67
Houston, Texas, 4, 158
Hughes, 26

I

IBM Corporation, 5
    employee involvement at, 22
    environmental leadership at, 168
    environmental policy of, 73, 168
    process redesign at, 109–10
    profitability of environmental
        steps at, 1, 11, 34–35
    recycling materials at, 140
    reducing consumption at, 122, 123,
        127
    reusing materials at, 5, 132, 133–
        34, 189
    suppliers and, 150
Ibuka, Masaru, 169
Inflammatory tactics, 38–39
Intel Corporation, 5
    employee involvement at, 51–52
    environmental leadership at, 168,
        173–74
    environmental policy of, 75
    organizational culture of, 179,
        181
    process redesign at, 112
    profitability of environmental
        steps at, 11, 38

    reducing consumption at, 5
    regional culture and, 182
    tracking environmental progress
        at, 58–59
ISO 14000, 22, 63, 67, 84–85, 90, 93,
    133, 151, 152, 172, 182, 201
ITT Cannon, 5
    customers' expectations and, 95
    employee involvement at, 5, 23
    environmental leadership at, 170–
        71
    profitability of environmental
        steps at, 9, 36, 37
    recycling materials at, 105, 139,
        141
    reducing consumption at, 9, 25–26,
        40–41, 125–26
    regional culture and, 182, 183
    reusing materials at, 129
ITT Gilfillan, 6
    customers' expectations and, 93
    environmental leadership at, 44,
        168
    process redesign at, 111–13
    profitability of environmental
        steps at, 14
ITT Industries, 37, 173
Izatt, Martin, 29, 36, 160–61, 164,
    197

J

Japan, customers' expectations in, 93
Jung, Claire, 120–21
Juran, Joseph, 183

K

Kaneko, Hisashi, 168
Kankyo Partners, 63
Klober, Linda, 125
Kubani, Dean, 53, 59–60, 126, 157,
    163, 199, 201, 202

Kyocera Corporation, 6
  eco-labels and, 98
  employee involvement at, 49
  green buildings and, 163
Kyocera Corporation *(continued)*
  green products of, 102, 104, 107
  process redesign at, 109
  profitability of environmental
    steps at, 35–36
  recycling materials at, 141
  suppliers and, 152

L

Labor, savings in, 16
Landscaping, 161
Larsen, Jim, 112
Latin America
  customers' expectations in,
    94
  regional culture of, 182
Lead, 124–26, 140
Leadership. *See* Environmental
  leadership
Lean and Green steps, 12, 19, 196.
  See also individual steps
Lean or Green myth, 1–3, 11, 13,
  150, 165, 195
Lear, David, 14, 154
Leibowitz, Alan, 37
Leypoldt, Mark, 159
Liability, avoiding, 14
Lighting, 158
Little, Barney, 43, 66, 119, 201
Los Angeles, California, 53, 126
Louisiana-Pacific Corporation, 6
  activists at, 188–89
  employee involvement at, 6, 46
  environmental leadership at, 169–
    70, 175–76
  environmental policy of, 74
  green products of, 10, 103

organizational culture of, 184–85
  recycling materials at, 138
LSI Logic Corporation, 6
  customers' expectations and, 92, 99
  employee involvement at, 25, 49
  environmental leadership at, 45
  environmental management
    system of, 85, 87
  environmental policy of, 77
  green buildings and, 158, 161,
    164
  profitability of environmental
    steps at, 8–9, 11
  public image and, 10–11
  recycling materials at, 137, 140,
    143
  reducing consumption at, 127, 143,
    197
  regional culture and, 182
  reusing materials at, 134–35, 143
  suppliers and, 149, 151, 156
  tracking environmental progress
    at, 60–61
Ludy, Perry J., 42
Lyon, Diana, 1, 109, 122, 150, 196

M

Management
  appealing to competitive spirit of,
    41
  convincing, 31–42, 135, 188–91
  starting with, 43–45
  using inflammatory tactics to
    pressure, 38–39
Martinez, Randall, 163
Martland, Danny, 13, 24, 46–47, 59,
  81, 84, 104, 134, 152, 164, 175,
  180, 190–91, 192, 198, 202–3
Matrix, 52
McIntosh, Ian, 83–84, 152, 153, 193
McKeown, Ian, 21, 44, 47, 60, 61, 68,

85, 93, 110, 122, 130–33, 135,
151, 189–90, 197
Media, involving, 53–54
Mexico, 94
Miho, Japan, 194
Mitchell, Chad, 140, 141
Mobers, Ton, 113–15
Mohin, Tim, 38, 59
Moore, Gordon, 168
Motorola, 132, 189
Moyer, Liz, 92, 190, 199

N
Natural Step Framework, 201
NEC Corporation, 6
  employee involvement at, 191
  environmental leadership at,
    168
  environmental management
    system of, 40, 84
  environmental policy of, 74, 77
  green products of, 147–48
  organizational culture of, 183
  profitability of environmental
    steps at, 6
  recycling materials at, 141–42
  suppliers and, 147–49, 150, 156
  tracking environmental progress
    at, 63, 64
New Zealand, 94
Nijmegen, Holland, 7, 113
Nokia, 73
North Pole, 2
Nozaki, Tadahiko, 40

O
Ohga, Norio, 169
Oil. *See also* Energy; Gas
  industry, 94
  recycling, 23
  reusing, 134

Organizational culture, 180–81, 183–
  86. *See also* Regional culture
O'Rourke, Frank, 14, 28, 51, 62, 95–
  96, 105, 150–51, 154–55, 193
Oseni, Martin, 35
Outsourcing, 152–53

P
Packaging
  recycling, 141
  reducing, 30, 121–22
  reusing, 9, 11–12, 23, 130–33,
    189
Paper
  recycling, 141
  reducing, 122
Paul, Idaho, 5, 174
Perfluorocarbons (PFCs), 112
Permit delays, avoiding, 106–7
Persistence, importance of, 189
Philips Electronics N. V., 7
  employee involvement at, 7, 22–
    23, 41, 50
  environmental leadership at, 172
  environmental policy of, 73, 74–75
  green products of, 13, 31, 103, 113–
    15
  profitability of environmental
    steps at, 9, 31
  reducing consumption at, 120
  reusing materials at, 9
  tracking environmental progress
    at, 63, 67
Plastic
  recycling, 141
  reusing, 134
Polaroid Corporation, 7
  activists at, 189
  customers' expectations and, 93
  employee involvement at, 21
  environmental leadership at, 44

Polaroid Corporation *(continued)*
  environmental management
    system of, 85, 86–87
  process redesign at, 110–11
  profitability of environmental
    steps at, 9, 11–12
  recycling materials at, 139, 189–90
  reducing consumption at, 7, 9, 122
  regional culture and, 47
  reusing materials at, 130–33, 135,
    189
  suppliers and, 151
  tracking environmental progress
    at, 60, 61, 68
Political groups, 39
Politics, playing, 189–90
Pollution, 53, 88, 126, 127
PricewaterhouseCoopers, 11
Process design, 110–13, 117
Product design, 113–15, 117
Product take-back, 142–43
Profitability
  increasing, 3, 8–11, 16
  myth of environment vs., 1–3, 11,
    13, 150, 165, 195
  tying environmental message to,
    32–33, 74
Public image, 10–11, 37–38, 106
Public transportation, 127, 128
Purchases, savings in, 15
Push system vs. pull system, 75

Q

Quality model, following, 183–85

R

Rae, Trevor, 73
Rauschhuber, Brian, 58, 138, 171–72
Recycling
  examples of, 8, 25, 37, 138–43
  motivating colleagues, 143–44

as part of RRR trilogy, 120, 137–
    38, 145
  revenue from, 105–6, 108, 137–38
Reducing
  examples of, 120–28
  as first choice, 120
  as part of RRR trilogy, 119, 145
Regional culture, 181–83
Reid, Harry, 26, 73, 148, 152, 187,
    201, 202
Reputation. *See* Public image
Return on investment, 35–36, 38, 42
Reusing
  convincing management and
    employees, 135
  examples of, 129–34
  importance of, 129
  as part of RRR trilogy, 119, 145
Revenues, increasing, 16, 101–8
Rider, Morgan, 149
Risk management, 37–38, 42
Rodriguez, Miguel Angel, 94
Roosevelt, Theodore, 171
Rosen, Len, 44
Rosenberg, Walt, 14, 28, 33–34, 44,
    47, 48, 57, 65, 66, 106, 149–150,
    192, 199, 201
RRR trilogy, 119–20, 145. *See also*
    Recycling; Reducing; Reusing

S

Sacramento, California, 4, 49, 138, 187
Sakumi, Hisashi, 109, 141
Samlesbury, England, 4, 10, 13, 47,
    180
San Francisco, California, 157
San Jose, California, 10–11
Santa Ana, California, 5
Santa Monica, California, 7
  green buildings and, 157, 160, 161–
    63

Natural Step Framework and, 201
public image of, 53–54
reducing consumption in, 10, 60,
  126, 127
regional culture and, 182–83
tracking environmental progress
  in, 59–60
Schomer, Dawne, 49, 106–7
Schubert, Sandra, 161–62
Scrap, recycling, 139
Sees, Jennifer, 175
Semiconductor industry, 10. *See also*
  individual companies
Shortsighted solutions, 40–41
Sierra Club, 53, 106
Singh, Nirmal, 25, 36, 37, 40, 105–6,
  125, 126, 129, 170–71, 182, 192
Smith, Liz, 74, 103, 176, 184, 185,
  186, 188, 192–93
Solder, 125–26
Solid waste, recycling, 138–39
Sony Corporation, 7
  employee involvement at, 191
  environmental leadership at, 169
  environmental policy of, 73, 77
  profitability of environmental
    steps at, 9
  recycling materials at, 7
  reducing consumption at, 9, 126,
    198
  tracking environmental progress
    at, 61
South Coast Air Quality
  Management District, 53
South Queensferry, Scotland, 4, 73,
  83, 159, 160, 197
Sowell, Shaunna, 23, 58, 61, 74, 123–
  24, 175, 183–84
Stangis, Dave, 38, 75, 168, 173, 199
"Stealing" ideas, 26, 52, 55
Superfund program, 94, 149, 169

Suppliers
  checking out suppliers of, 154–55
  cost and, 150–51
  educating, 152
  outsourcing and, 152–53
  rating, by green practices, 148–50
  taking a hard stance with, 151–52
  waste-disposal, 149–50
Sustainability, 94, 168, 200–2
Suwyn, Mark, 185
Swinford, Byron, 91

T
Taguchi, Genichi, 183
Taiwan, 93
Takagi, Noriko, 194
Taylor, Chuck, 95
Tenore, Ann, 143–44
Terrell, Billy, 174
Texas Instruments Incorporated, 8
  avoiding loss of potential revenues,
    106–7
  customers' expectations and, 92
  employee involvement at, 49
  environmental leadership at, 175
  environmental management
    system of, 84
  environmental policy of, 71, 72, 74,
    75–76, 77–78
  green buildings and, 159
  organizational culture of, 183–84
  process redesign at, 115–16
  profitability of environmental
    steps at, 8, 23
  recycling materials at, 25, 140, 141
  reducing consumption at, 120–21,
    123–24, 127
  reusing materials at, 23
  tracking environmental progress
    at, 58–59, 61–63
Thomson Multimedia, 8

Thomson Multimedia *(continued)*
  customers' expectations and, 97–98
  eco-labels and, 97–98
  environmental leadership at, 172,
    174
  environmental management
    system of, 84–85, 87–89
  environmental policy of, 72, 77
  green products of, 106
  process redesign at, 89, 109
  profitability of environmental
    steps at, 9
  recycling materials at, 139, 141,
    143
  reducing consumption at, 8, 27,
    121–22
  reusing materials at, 134
  tracking environmental progress
    at, 60, 64–65
Tokyo, Japan, 6, 7
Toronto, Canada, 4, 161
Transportation costs, reducing, 15, 115
Travis, Lauri, 169

U
United States
  customers' expectations in, 93–94
  regional culture of, 182–83
U.S. Environmental Protection
    Agency
  Energy Star, 93, 96, 97

  fines from, 184–85
  Superfund, 94, 149

V
Van Nuys, California, 6
Violence, 39
Vision, importance of, 171–72

W
Waste-disposal suppliers, 149–50
Wasteful practices, questioning, 21–
    30
Water conservation, 88–89, 110,
    120–21, 134–35, 141, 160–61
Watson, Thomas J., Jr., 168
Whistle-blowing, 53–54
White-top, 7, 160
Willamette Industries, 185
World Environment Center, 41

Y
Yasu, Japan, 110
Yeakley, Tim, 28, 140

Z
Zehnder, Bill, 53, 191
Zeilinski, Tom, 93, 111, 168
Zelayeta, Joe, 10
Zyrardow, Poland, 27

Pamela J. Gordon is a leader and speaker in the worlds of business, professional associations, political parties, and education. She is president and founder of Technology Forecasters, Inc., a management consulting firm that for four years in a row was named by the *San Francisco Business Times* as one of the 100 fastest growing private companies in the Bay Area. Her firm, with a staff of 40 people, helps high-tech industry executives around the globe "turn insight into profitability." Clients include Siemens, Motorola, Orient Semiconductor Electronics, Agilent Technologies, Solectron Corporation, Agile Software, and the Canadian government.

Executives worldwide know Ms. Gordon for her expertise in manufacturing efficiency and business strategy. She has managed benchmark studies comparing companies' environmental compliance, quality, human resources, marketing strategy, and other business issues. Her business and environmental insights have been quoted in *Fortune* magazine, the *Wall Street Journal*, and other publications around the world, and she has appeared numerous times on television and radio.

Ms. Gordon is an environmentalist at heart. Since she was eight years old, the Gordon family has gone backpacking in California's mountain ranges and paddled down Western U.S. rivers. Ms. Gordon is a long-time contributor to several environmental organizations, and for many years Technology Forecasters—itself a Lean and Green company—has donated 5 percent of its profits to environmental organizations.

Gordon is a Certified Management Consultant, certified by the Institute of Management Consultants. She was President of the Northern California Chapter. An avid speaker, Ms. Gordon speaks at corporate meetings, association conferences, and universities internationally.

Pamela Gordon can be contacted by e-mail at Pgordon@TechForecast ers.com, by phone at 510-747-1900, or through Berrett-Koehler Publishers, 235 Montgomery Street, Suite 650, San Francisco, CA 94104-2916 USA (tel. 415-288-0260).